Keto Meal Prep

A Complete Keto Beginners Guide with 100 Easy and Scrumptious Keto Meal Prep Recipes and 28-Days Keto Meal Plan for Rapid Weight Loss and Good Health

Dolores Hearn

ISBN-13: 979-8666224199

DEDICATION

To all who desire to live life to the fullest!

TABLE OF CONTENT

INTRODUCTION

The ketogenic diet is not just another weight loss diet. For many, it is a special diet that has become a lifestyle with records of all-round sterling results. The little additional work of planning and preparing your ketogenic snacks and meals up front will be the major strategy needed that defines your level of success on the diet; also helping you remain in ketosis. The biggest pay-off of planning and making your ketogenic meals and snacks ahead is the drastic reduction of the temptation to reach for sugar and carb-filled foods or snacks.

We love the ketogenic diet, but it can be overwhelming sticking to a restrictive diet like the keto diet without a formidable plan. The saying "nothing worth having comes easy" applies in this case. Learning to plan and prep your keto meals will help you scale through the difficulty associated with starting out on new health diets. In this cookbook, you will find and prepare delicious meals and snacks that you will want to eat repeatedly. Also, you will discover money-saving tips, and essential kitchen tools for easier meal prep, and the basics of ketogenic meal preparation.

This cookbook will help you reach your intended health and fitness goals, and also help you reach and remain in ketosis. Similarly, you will exploit the various benefits of the ketogenic diet, such as: improved PCOS symptoms, potentially reduced seizures, protected brain function, improved heart health, reduced risk to some types of cancers, improved acne, lowered inflammation, increased energy, stabilized blood sugar, and enhanced weight loss. What's more? you will enjoy a variety of healthy foods that are keto friendly, more so keto meal prepping opens you up to a world of an unparalleled-keto-deliciousness.

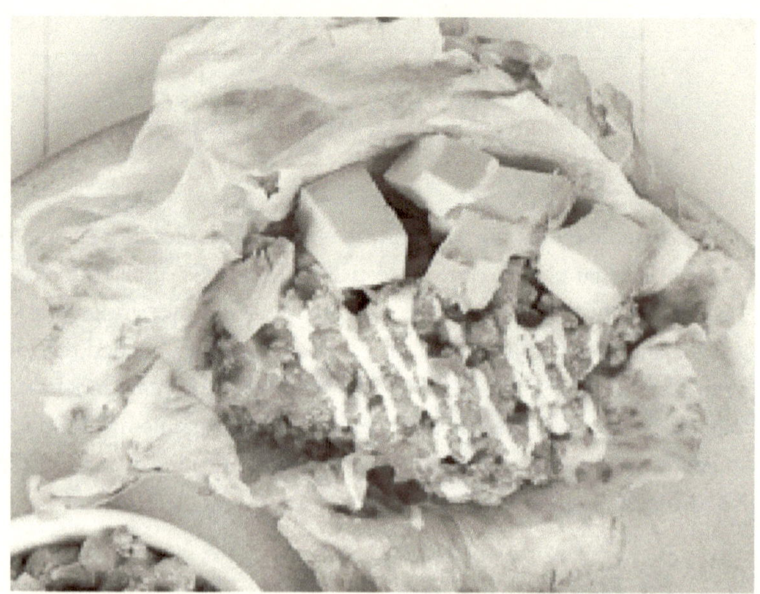

This part contains a detailed keto meal preparation guide, as well as a 28-day meal plan to help you prepare your keto meals and snacks effortlessly. The good thing is that you will learn and become better on the job. The more meals you prep, the more proficient and comfortable you become. In addition, the meal plan is not set in stone, you can make little adjustments frequently, as you settle into a comfortable routine of meal prepping your meals weekly.

A BEGINNER'S GUIDE TO KETO MEAL PREPPING

The ketogenic diet offers an endless list of food options that every keto dieter can choose from. Each keto-dieter can consume from these high fat and low carb food options: fats, oils, keto-friendly 'low carb' sweeteners (like stevia, monk fruit, erythritol), berries, avocado, seeds, nuts, high-fat dairy, above ground veggies (such as green beans, asparagus, and broccoli), leafy greens, fish and meat. Foods, such as tubers (like sweet potatoes, and yam), sugar and grains are discouraged on the diet.

With all that in mind, the ketogenic diet demands some amount of effort and time to prep your meals, and to ensure a successful move into ketosis. This guide has been provided for a smooth and hassle-free ride, and to help you stick to the ketogenic diet as you take your first baby steps!

Basic Pantry Staples

The following ingredients should be kept within reach for easy prepping of most of your keto recipes when needed.

Coconut oil

Olive oil

Avocado oil

Olive oil

Coconut aminos

Nut-based butters

Garlic (cloves and powder)

Toasted and/or raw nuts (almonds, pistachios, etc.)

Baking powder and baking soda

Seeds and nuts

Almond and coconut flour

Salt & pepper

Cilantro

Dill

Tarragon

Parsley

Oregano

Celery salt

MCT oil powder

Thyme

Red wine vinegar

Cocoa powder

Keto-friendly sweeteners, such as monk fruit and stevia

Sun-dried tomatoes

Pumpkin pie spice

Coconut flour

Almond flour

Vanilla extract

Cinnamon

Red pepper flakes

Yellow or Dijon mustard

Basic Refrigerator and Freezer Staples
Cream cheese

Full-fat coconut milk or heavy cream

Guacamole or avocado

Keto-friendly mayonnaise

Eggs

Plain unsweetened yogurt or sour cream

Preferred fish (cod, tuna, salmon, halibut etc.)

Keto friendly salad dressings

Beef

Hot sauce

Sausage or bacon

Keto-friendly ketchup

Almond or coconut milk

Coconut aminos

Zucchini

Spinach

Butter

Any of your favorite cheeses

Cheese sticks

Riced cauliflower

Important Keto Equipment and Tools

These are essential tools and equipment that will save you time in the coming weeks and they are needed for your keto meal prep success.

The Right Meal Prep Containers. Your meal prep containers should be same size for easy stacking, with well-fitted lid and should be preferably glass (since they can be heated). These will keep your prepped meals fresh all week long. Rightly portion your prepped meals into these airtight containers after meal prepping, and store as necessary.

Parchment Paper. The parchment paper is an important means to prevent joining when you bake. It works well on a baking pan or in a casserole dish.

Baking Sheet. These are important tools for roasting or baking your veggies, marinated protein and other oven-baked meals. Invest in buying good sheet pans, they will come in handy.

Vegetable Spiralizer. This tool will help you make veggie noodles in the comfort of your kitchen, while cutting down on the cost of buying pre-spiralized vegetables at the grocery store. You are also likely to buy fresh and better vegetable produce at the farmer's market.

Electric Pressure Cooker or Slow Cooker. The electric pressure cooker is a useful equipment to make homemade soups and broths quickly. The slow cooker is also an important kitchen equipment that is just right for "set and forget" meals.

Handheld Blenders. This equipment is useful for whipping cream, keto-friendly mayonnaise, making sauces, blending broth and beating eggs. They are easy to handle and pocket-friendly.

Muffin tins. These is also an important tool needed to prepare most breakfast recipes. You can fill your muffin cups with several things, such as meats, fish fillets, veggies and every dessert. You can buy silicone (non-stick) ones or the regular metal muffin tins.

Blender or Food Processor. An electric blender or food processor can help to make your delicious coffee drinks, smoothies, salad dressings, nut butters and riced cauliflower that are all keto-friendly.

Filet Knife and/or Chef's Knife. For an effective meal prep, a good knife is very essential for all the slicing, dicing, chopping and cutting. Make sure you use only high-quality knives to avoid potential danger associated with cheap knives.

Skillet. Buy a cast-iron skillet. This type of skillet is safe, easy to clean and long lasting.

Easy Meal Prep Strategy

There is no "one rule fits all" principle for keto meal preparation. You may have heard the saying "less is more", hence the need to start simple, you need to keep in mind. With continuous practice you will find your meal preparation rhythm and discover what works for you. Here is a guide to help you get started.

Make a Decision. Pick a day in a week to decide on and write down your plan for the next one week. Estimate the number of people and meals per day for that particular week, breakfast, main course, desserts and snacks. Outline them and plan whether or not you want new meals per day or leftovers from the day before. You can have same meals twice or more by doubling a recipe. Account for the recipes and the ingredients needed to make each recipe in details.

Choose a day or days to shop for groceries and also for prepping your keto meals and snacks. You can shop for groceries in a day and prep the other day, or you can do all in one day. Stick with what works for you. Also, start with simple recipes with a small number of ingredients, and look for recipes that have comparable ingredients, like veggies and meat. It helps to make your shopping and cooking faster and easier.

Compiling your List and Shopping. Make your list by compiling ingredients from each recipe you have decided to cook for the week. Group your ingredients into categories for easier access at the store and for smart shopping. Your shopping list should include the precise quantity of ingredient needed for each recipe, and for the week's meal prep, and make sure you stick to your shopping list. In addition, buy whole foods, such as veggies, eggs and meat. And avoid pre-packaged products that are labelled as "keto". Also, buy from the produce and butcher sections of the store for fresh ingredients.

Preparing Your meals. Yaay! it's time to cook. This can be slightly overwhelming when starting, but it will become easier as you prep more. Place every ingredient needed for your meal prep on a work surface or table for easy access and to save time. Prep meats and other proteins and chop your vegetables before you begin to cook. Also, go over your plan and your recipes, and work out which steps take more time. Start with those steps. For instance, if you have to rice your cauliflower, and cook turkey in a slow cooker for one recipe; start with slow cooking the turkey before prepping the cauliflower rice.

Divide cooked and cooled meals into well sectioned and airtight containers with lid and store appropriately. In addition, you should label each meal prep container with a sticky paper, and note the date of preparation, the macros, day of the week the meal is for and so on.

Start meal prepping your keto meals today and you will enjoy a better, healthier, and longer life. Cheers!

28-DAY MEAL PLAN

1st Day

Breakfast: Pepper Ring (Breakfast Keto)pg 19

Lunch: Brussel Sprouts Bacon Au Gratinpg 103

Dinner: Chinese Hot & Sour Souppg 111

Evening Snack: DeliciousParmesan Cheddar Crispspg 149

2nd Day

Breakfast: Vanilla Pumpkin Muffinspg 21, plus coffee (add 2 tablespoons heavy cream)

Lunch: Cheesy Bacon Jalapeno Popperspg 91

Dinner: Scrumptious Keto Steak Fajitaspg 113

Evening Snack: A few apple slices with peanut butter

3rd Day

Breakfast: Keto Cream Cheese Pancakespg 22

Lunch: Keto Buffalo Turkey Meatballspg 89, with your favorite keto salad

Dinner: Slow Cooker Beef Soup Recipepg 114, plus keto (low-carb) crackers

Evening Snack: 1/2 avocado, sprinkled with pepper and salt

4th Day

Breakfast: Egg Sausage Sandwich (Breakfast Keto)pg 23

Lunch: Keto Chicken Jar Saladpg 88

Dinner: Mozzarella Pizza Casserolepg 117

Evening Snack: Preferred Berries with coconut cream

5th Day

Breakfast: Keto Spinach Bacon Frittatapg 25

Lunch: Chicken Fajitas (Keto Sheet Pan)pg 87

Dinner: Slow Cooker Chicken Buffalo Souppg 116, plus keto (low-carb) crackers

Evening Snack: Cheesy Ham Roll upspg 153

6th Day

Breakfast: Keto Zucchini Bagelspg 26, plus coffee (add 2 tablespoons heavy cream)

Lunch: Fennel Asparagus Salmon Bakepg 85

Dinner: Italian Cheesy Eggplant Lasagnapg 119

Evening Snack: Kale Chips with Nutritional Yeastpg 158

7th Day

Breakfast: Creamy French Crepespg 27

Lunch: Zoodle Chicken Keto Capresepg 83

Dinner: Low Carb Fathead Pizza Crustpg 121, with desired keto toppings

Evening Snack:<u>Keto Cheese Peach Danishpg 159</u>

8th Day

Breakfast: <u>Yummy Cloud Bread (Morning Keto)pg 29</u>, plus coffee (add 2 tablespoons heavy cream)

Lunch:<u>Chicken Breast Bakepg 82</u>

Dinner:<u>Keto Cream of Mushroom Souppg 123</u>, plus keto (low-carb) crackers

Evening Snack: A few raw almonds

9th Day

Breakfast:<u>Cheddar BreakfastCasserolepg 32</u>

Lunch:<u>Cheese Chicken Caesar Saladpg 80</u>

Dinner:<u>Tasty Shredded Chicken Soup with Spaghetti Squashpg 124</u>

Evening Snack:<u>Frenchliver Patepg 163</u>

10th Day

Breakfast:<u>Glazed Lime Zucchini Breadpg 33</u>, plus coffee (add 2 tablespoons heavy cream)

Lunch:<u>Keto Chicken Bacon Shellspg 79</u>

Dinner:<u>Tasty Beef Chilipg 125</u>, plus keto (low-carb) crackers

Evening Snack: <u>Ketogenic White Trufflespg 169</u>

11th Day
Breakfast: Keto Zucchini Pizza Muffinspg 35

Lunch: Tasty Bacon Chicken Casserolepg 77

Dinner: SlowCooker Chuck Roast Recipepg 127

Evening Snack: Roasted Fish Rouladepg 161

12th Day
Breakfast: Yummy Baked Almond Flour Bread with Bananapg 30

Lunch: Cauliflower Chicken Bakepg 75

Dinner: BeefyCauliflower Casserolepg 128

Evening Snack: Keto Egg Muffinspg 154

13th Day
Breakfast: Keto Bacon Spinach Quiche (without Crust)pg 37

Lunch: Delicious Baked Peri Peri Chickenpg 73

Dinner: Chicken Coconut Currypg 131

Evening Snack: Cheesy Ham Roll upspg 153

14th Day
Breakfast: Ketogenic Fathead Bagelspg 38, plus coffee (add 2 tablespoons heavy cream)

Lunch: Fried Cauliflower Rice with Steakpg 70

Dinner: Kale Turkey Souppg 133, plus keto (low-carb) crackers

Evening Snack: A few celery sticks with nut-based butter

15th Day

Breakfast: <u>Creamy Banana Muffin with Nutspg 40</u>

Lunch: <u>Almond Flour Meatloafpg 69</u>

Dinner: <u>Coodles with Roasted Fennel Salmonpg 135</u>

Evening Snack: <u>Crumbly ToppedPie Cupcakespg 164</u>

16th Day

Breakfast:<u>Rosemary Cauliflower Breadpg 42</u>

Lunch: <u>Keto ColeslawRecipepg 67</u>

Dinner:<u>Ketogenic Chicken Salsa Souppg 136</u>, plus keto (low-carb) crackers

Evening Snack: <u>Ketogenic White Trufflespg 169</u>

17th Day

Breakfast: <u>Simple andTasty Egg Muffinspg 44</u>

Lunch: <u>Keto Jalapeno Cornbread Muffinspg 66</u>

Dinner:<u>Keto Cheesy Lasagna Noodlespg 138</u>

Evening Snack: Pork rinds

18th Day

Breakfast: <u>Peppered Cheese Keto Pizza (Breakfast)pg 45</u>

Lunch:<u>Filled Keto Tortillas with Spicy Saucepg 64</u>

Dinner:<u>Cauliflower Cheddar Casserolepg 140</u>

Evening Snack: A few celery sticks with nut-based butter

19th Day

Breakfast:<u>Creamy Banana Muffin with Nutspg 40</u>, plus coffee (add 2 tablespoons heavy cream)

Lunch: <u>Filled PepperLasagnapg 62</u>

Dinner: <u>Keto Oxtail Stewpg 142</u>

Evening Snack: Coconut chips

20th Day

Breakfast: <u>Keto Spinach Bacon Frittatapg 25</u>

Lunch: <u>Keto Spinach Filled Salmon Bakepg 60</u>

Dinner:<u>Caribbean Keto Pepper Potpg 144</u>

Evening Snack: <u>Crumbly Topped Pie Cupcakespg 164</u>

21st Day

Breakfast: <u>Keto Zucchini Pizza Muffinspg 35</u>

Lunch:<u>Keto Crack Slaw with Porkpg 58</u>

Dinner: <u>Mongolian Keto Beefpg 147</u>

Evening Snack: Macadamia nuts

22nd Day
Breakfast: <u>Simple and Tasty Egg Muffinspg 44</u>, plus coffee (add 2 tablespoons heavy cream)

Lunch: <u>Buttery Crab Filled Salmonpg 56</u>

Dinner: <u>Cauliflower Cheddar Casserolepg 140</u>

Evening Snack:<u>Keto-Japanese Sushi Rollspg 150</u>

23rd Day
Breakfast:<u>Peppered Cheese Keto Pizza (Breakfast)pg 45</u>

Lunch:<u>Tzatziki Sauced Meatballs (Keto Mediterranean)pg 54</u>

Dinner: <u>Ketogenic Chicken Salsa Souppg 136</u>, plus keto (low-carb) crackers

Evening Snack: Coconut chips

24th Day
Breakfast:<u>Creamy French Crepespg 27</u>, plus coffee (add 2 tablespoons heavy cream)

Lunch:<u>Mexican Beef Taco Saladpg 53</u>

Dinner:<u>Coodles with Roasted Fennel Salmonpg 135</u>

Evening Snack: Pork rinds

25th Day
Breakfast:<u>Keto Zucchini Bagelspg 26</u>, plus coffee (add 2 tablespoons heavy cream)

Lunch:<u>Keto Turkey Burgerspg 50</u>

Dinner: Tasty Beef Chilipg 125

Evening Snack: A few celery sticks with nut-based butter

26th Day
Breakfast: CheddarBreakfast Casserolepg 32

Lunch: Keto Tuna Saladpg 51

Dinner: Italian Cheesy Eggplant Lasagnapg 119

Evening Snack: Macadamia nuts

27th Day
Breakfast: Keto Bacon Spinach Quiche (without Crust)pg 37

Lunch: Keto Hamburger Bunspg 48

Dinner: Chinese Hot & Sour Souppg 111, plus keto (low-carb) crackers

Evening Snack: A few celery sticks with nut-based butter

28th Day
Breakfast: Pepper Ring (Breakfast Keto)pg 19 , plus coffee (add 2 tablespoons heavy cream)

Lunch: Keto Cauliflower Egg Saladpg 47

Dinner: Tasty Beef Chilipg 125

Evening Snack: Bacon, cooked

BREAKFAST

Pepper Ring (Breakfast Keto)

Preparation Time: 10 minutes

Cook Time: 10 minutes

Serves: 4 servings

Ingredients

Pepper

Salt

Coconut Oil

4 tablespoons parmesan cheese (shredded)

1 pound breakfast sausage

8 eggs

2 red bell peppers (slice top & remove the seeds)

Directions

1. Place a small pan over med-heat and add in the sausage.

2. Cook the sausage until it is brown. Drain the cooked sausage and let stand.

3. Cut each red bell pepper into four rings (total of 8 rings).

4. At med-high heat, place a pan over heat and add coconut oil (2 tablespoons).

5. Add the 8 pepper rings into the pan and saute while coconut oil heats.

6. Gently crack an egg into each pepper ring when the coconut oil begins to sizzle.

Note: The egg may overflow or leak.

7. Season each pepper ring with pepper and salt.

8. Top each yolk with cooked sausage (2 tablespoons).

9. Cook the eggs in the rings until it is well cooked as desired.

Nutritional Information/Serving

Calories 483 kcal, Protein 25g, Sugar 4g, Dietary Fiber 1g, Net Carbs 5g Carbohydrates 6g, Total Fat 40g

Vanilla Pumpkin Muffins

Preparation Time: 10 minutes

Cook Time: 25 minutes

Serves: 10 servings

Ingredients

Pumpkin seeds

1 teaspoon vanilla extract

1/2 cup coconut oil

3/4 cup pumpkin puree

4 large eggs

1/4 teaspoon sea salt

1 tablespoon pumpkin pie spice

1 tablespoon baking powder

2/3 cup sweetener

1/2 cup sunflower seed meal

1/2 cup coconut flour

Directions

1. Use parchment paper to line 10 muffin cups and heat up the oven to 350°F.

2. Add salt, pumpkin pie spice, baking powder, sweetener, sunflower seed meal and coconut flour into a big bowl.

3. Stir the coconut flour mixture together until a smooth texture is formed.

4. Add in vanilla extract, coconut oil, pumpkin puree and eggs into the coconut flour mixture.

5. Stir until a smooth texture is reached.

6. Share the batter among the prepared muffin cups evenly.

7. Fill each cup, 2/3 of the cup and use a spoon to smooth the out the top of the batter in each muffin cup.

8. Top the batter with pumpkin seeds by sprinkling.

9. Press the pumpkin seeds lightly into the batter.

10. Transfer the muffin cups into the oven and bake until muffins are lightly browned at the ends, for 25 minutes.

Nutritional Information/Serving

Calories 173 kcal, Dietary Fiber 3g, Net Carbs 4g, Protein 4g, Fat 14g

Keto Cream Cheese Pancakes
Preparation Time: 5 minutes

Cook Time: 5 minutes

Serves: 2 servings

Ingredients

1/2 teaspoon vanilla extract

1/2 teaspoon baking powder

1 tablespoon sweetener

2 tablespoons heavy cream

3 tablespoons coconut flour

2 ounces (softened at room temperature) cream cheese

2 large egg

Directions

1. In an electric blender, add vanilla extract, baking powder, sweetener, heavy cream, coconut flour, cream cheese and eggs.

2. Blend the coconut flour mixture until a fine texture is formed.

3. Set aside the batter to thicken lightly for some minutes.

4. At med-heat, place a buttered pan over heat and add the batter into the pan.

5. Fry the pancakes in the pan for a minute or 2 minutes on each side.

Note: Turn the pancake when bubbles are formed at the ends of each pancake.

6. Repeat the process above with the remaining batter.

Nutritional Information/Serving

Calories 267 kcal, Dietary Fiber 3g, Net Carbs 4g, Protein 9g, Fat 21g

Egg Sausage Sandwich (Breakfast Keto)

Preparation Time: 5 minutes

Cook Time: 10 minutes

Serves: 1 serving

Ingredients

Avocado (a few slices)

2 sharp cheddar cheese (sliced)

2 (cooked) sausage patties

1 tablespoon mayo

2 large eggs

1 tablespoon butter

Directions

1. On med-heat, place a big pan over heat and add in a tablespoon of butter.

2. Lightly grease 2 silicone egg molds and place it into the pan with the butter.

3. Crack 2 large eggs into the egg molds and whisk gently with a fork.

4. Place lid over the pan and cook the eggs until is well cooked, for 3 minutes to 4 minutes.

5. Take the eggs from the silicone egg molds, transfer an egg onto a plate and garnish with 1/2 tbsp of mayo.

6. Add a sausage patty to top the egg in the plate.

7. Add avocado slices and cheddar cheese over the top of the sausage patty.

8. On the avocado slices, add the other sausage patty and top with the remaining cheddar cheese.

9. On the second cooked egg, add 1/2 tablespoon of mayo and spread.

10. Place the second egg with the mayo on the cheddar cheese layer and serve.

Nutritional Information/Serving

Calories 880 kcal, Protein 32g, Dietary Fiber 2g, Carbohydrates 8g, Fat 82g, Net Carbs 6g

Keto Spinach Bacon Frittata

Preparation Time: 10 minutes

Cook Time: 20 minutes

Serves: 3 servings

Ingredients

1 chopped, rosemary sprig

2 cups (steamed & coarsely chopped) collard greens

1 1/2 cups (cooked & divide into half) green beans

4 oz (slice into 1/2" pieces) pasture-raised bacon

1 tbsp ghee

8 eggs

Directions

1. Heat up a fan assisted oven to 350°F.

2. At med-heat, place a 12" oven-safe saucepan over heat, add rosemary sprig, bacon and ghee.

3. Saute until bacon is crisped lightly for 3 minutes.

4. Add collard greens and green beans into the saucepan. Saute until the collard greens becomes tender.

5. In a small bowl, add the eggs and beat. Pour the whisked eggs into the pan. For 5 minutes, saute until the sides and the lower part are cooked.

6. Move the saucepan into the preheated oven and bake until the frittata is cooked through for 5 minutes.

7. Take the pan out of the oven and set aside to cool.

8. Divide frittata into 3 parts and add salad when ready to serve.

Nutritional Information/Serving

Calories 413 kcal, Protein 22.6g, Carbs 5.3g, Fat 33.7g

Keto Zucchini Bagels

Preparation Time: 15 minutes

Cook Time: 20 minutes

Serves: 4 servings

Ingredients

1/4 teaspoon sea salt

1 teaspoon baking powder

2 large eggs

1/3 cup coconut flour

1 cup (shredded) mozzarella cheese

3 zucchini (medium)

Directions

1. Heat up the oven to 400°F.

2. In a food processor, add the zucchini and shred. Transfer the shredded zucchini into a colander.

3. Lightly sprinkle salt over the shredded zucchini and set aside to drain, for 20 minutes or at most 1 hour.

4. On a cheese cloth, transfer the drained zucchini, and squeeze until the remaining moisture is drained.

5. Add the shredded mozzarella cheese into a small bowl, and microwave cheese for 1 minute and 30 seconds.

6. In a big bowl, add baking powder, eggs and coconut flour. Mix together.

7. Add in the microwaved mozzarella cheese into the coconut flour bowl.

8. Use hands to knead dough until a fine texture is reached.

9. Use olive oil to spray a silicone bagel mold and transfer the dough into the mold.

10. Gently press the dough with hand into the cavities.

11. Transfer the mold into the oven and bake until it is golden for 15 minutes to 20 minutes.

Nutritional Information/Serving

Calories 176 kcal, Dietary Fiber 7g, Net Carbs 7g, Protein 15g, Fat 10g

Creamy French Crepes

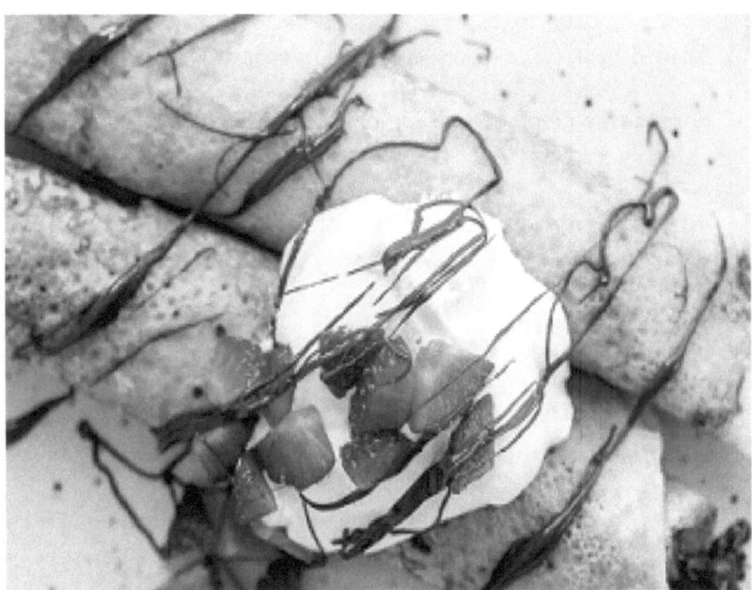

Preparation Time: 5 minutes

Cook Time: 10 minutes

Serves: 4 servings

Ingredients

1/4 teaspoon vanilla extract

1/2 teaspoon cinnamon

Sea salt (a pinch)

1 teaspoon erythritol

1/4 cup mascarpone

2 large eggs

Directions

1. In a food processor, add vanilla extract, cinnamon, salt, erythritol, mascarpone and eggs.

2. Process until a fine texture is formed.

3. At med-heat, place a greased skillet over heat.

4. Form a thin crepe by swirling batter (1/4 cup) on a greased skillet over the heat.

5. Saute until bubbles starts to form at the crepe ends, for a minute to 2 minutes.

6. Turn the crepe and saute on the other side, for a minute.

7. Repeat the process above with the remaining batter.

Nutritional Information/Serving

Calories 99 kcal, Dietary Fiber 0.3g, Net Carbs 0.7g, Protein 4g, Fat 9g

Yummy Cloud Bread (Morning Keto)

Preparation Time: 10 minutes

Cook Time: 25 minutes

Serves: 6 servings

Ingredients

1/8 teaspoon sea salt

1/8 teaspoon cream of tartar

3 ounces cream cheese

3 large (Separate the yolks and whites) eggs

Directions

1. Use parchment paper to line a baking pan and lightly grease the parchment paper.

2. Heat up the oven to 300°F.

3. Add cream of tartar and egg whites into a big bowl.

4. Beat the egg white mixture with an electric mixer, until it forms stiff peaks.

5. Add salt, egg yolks and cream cheese into another big bowl. Beat until a fine texture is formed.

6. Use a spatula to fold in the egg-whites mixture into the cream cheese mixture.

7. Combine the mixture in a folding motion.

8. On the prepared baking pan, add mixture and form into 6 circular discs.

9. Transfer the pan into the oven and bake until it is browned, for 25 minutes to 35 minutes.

Nutritional Information/Serving

Calories 98 kcal, Dietary Fiber 0g, Net Carbs 0.2g, Protein 4g, Fat 9g

Yummy Baked Almond Flour Bread with Banana

Preparation Time: 10 minutes

Cook Time: 1 hour

Serves: 12 servings

Ingredients

2 teaspoons banana extract

1/4 cup almond milk (unsweetened)

4 large egg

1/2 cup erythritol

6 tablespoons coconut oil

1/4 teaspoon sea salt

2 teaspoons cinnamon

2 teaspoons baking powder

1 cup (chopped) walnuts

1/4 cup coconut flour

2 cups almond flour (blanched)

Directions

1. Use parchment paper to line a loaf pan of 5 by 9", and heat up the oven to 350°F.

Note: For easy removal, the parchment paper should hang over the 2 opposite sides of the loaf pan.

2. Add salt, cinnamon, baking powder, coconut flour and almond flour into a big bowl. Mix together.

3. Add erythritol and coconut oil into another big bowl.

4. Beat the coconut oil mixture with a hand mixer until it is fluffy.

5. Whisk in the 4 large eggs and beat on low.

6. Stir in the unsweetened almond milk and banana extract.

7. Pour egg mixture into the almond flour bowl and use hand mixer to beat until a doughy texture is reached, on low speed.

8. Add in 1/2 cup of walnuts and stir lightly.

9. Add the batter into the prepared loaf pan and use the back of a spoon to smooth out the top, by evenly pressing into the batter.

10. Top batter with more walnuts as needed and lightly press down into the batter.

11. Place the loaf pan into the oven, and bake until a toothpick inserted comes out clean, for 50 minutes to 60 minutes.

12. Set aside the banana bread to cool completely, slice and serve.

Nutritional Information/Serving

Calories 224 kcal, Dietary Fiber 4g, Net Carbs 2g, Protein 8g, Fat 20g

Cheddar Breakfast Casserole

Preparation Time: 5 minutes

Cook Time: 40 minutes

Serves: 9 servings

Ingredients

1/4 tsp black pepper

1/4 teaspoon sea salt

2 tablespoons (chopped) fresh parsley

2 cups cheddar cheese

1/2 cup heavy cream

12 large eggs

6 cloves (minced) garlic

1 pound breakfast sausage

Directions

1. At med-high heat, grease a pan and place it over heat.

2. Add garlic and saute until aromatic, for 1 minute.

3. Add in sausage, use spatula to break apart and saute until it is golden, for 10 minutes.

4. Heat up the oven to 375°F.

5. Add black pepper, salt, parsley, 1 cup of cheddar cheese, heavy cream and eggs into a big bowl. Whisk together.

6. Grease the base of a glass casserole dish of 9 by 9".

7. Add in the cooked sausage into the greased dish and evenly arrange.

8. Transfer the egg mixture into the dish and pour it over the sausage.

9. Sprinkle 1 cup of cheddar cheese over the egg mixture.

10. Transfer the dish into the oven and bake until the cheese melts and the eggs are baked, for 30 minutes.

Nutritional Information/Serving

Calories 281 kcal, Dietary Fiber 0.1g, Net Carbs 0.9g, Protein 17g, Fat 23g

Glazed Lime Zucchini Bread

Preparation Time: 15 minutes

Cook Time: 1 hour

Serves: 18 servings

Ingredients

1 cup blueberries

1 1/2 cup (grated) zucchini

1/4 teaspoon sea salt

2 teaspoons baking powder

2 cups almond flour (blanched)

1 teaspoon vanilla extract

1 tablespoon lime zest

1 tablespoon lime juice

3 large egg

3/4 cup erythritol

1/2 cup (softened) butter

Lime glaze

4 teaspoons lime juice

1/4 cup sweetener (powdered)

Directions

1. Use parchment paper to line a loaf pan of 5 by 9", and heat up the oven to 325°F.

2. Add erythritol and butter into a big bowl. Beat the butter mixture together until it becomes fluffy.

3. Add vanilla extract, lime zest, lime juice and eggs into another bowl and beat.

4. Pour the egg mixture into the erythritol bowl.

5. In another bowl, add salt, baking powder and almond flour.

6. Mix the almond flour mixture until combined and transfer it into the erythritol bowl.

7. Use cheesecloth to wrap the zucchini and squeeze to drain the moisture.

8. Transfer the squeezed zucchini into the batter and stir until combined.

9. Fold berries into the batter mixture.

10. In the lined loaf pan, transfer the batter and use a spatula to smooth out the upper part of the batter.

11. Transfer the pan into the oven and bake the batter for 60 minutes to 70 minutes.

Note: Check for doneness by inserting a toothpick.

12. Set aside the pan until bread is cool.

13. Add the powdered sweetener and lime juice into a bowl and whisk together to make the lime glaze.

14. Dribble the lime glaze over the baked berry zucchini bread.

Nutritional Information/Serving

Calories 139 kcal, Dietary Fiber 2g, Net Carbs 3g, Protein 4g, Fat 12g

Keto Zucchini Pizza Muffins

Preparation Time: 15 minutes

Cook Time: 20 minutes

Serves: 10 servings

Ingredients

1 tablespoon (melted) butter

2 large egg

1/4 teaspoon black pepper

1/2 teaspoon sea salt

2 tablespoons coconut flour

1 1/4 cup (shredded) mozzarella cheese

2 medium (shredded) zucchinis

Topping

1 ounce (slice into quarters) pepperoni mini slices

1 teaspoon Italian seasoning

2/3 cup (shredded) mozzarella cheese

1/4 cup marinara sauce

Directions

1. Use silicone liner to line a mini muffin pan of 20 cups and heat up the oven to 375°F.

2. Add black pepper, salt, coconut flour, mozzarella cheese and zucchini into a big bowl. Stir together.

3. Add the butter and eggs into the zucchini bowl and stir together.

4. Evenly divide the zucchini mixture among the prepared muffin cups and flatten the top with the back of a spoon.

5. Transfer the muffin pan into the oven and bake until the upper part is solid and brown, for 18 minutes to 22 minutes.

Note: In case the muffins puff up, use the back of a spoon to flatten and set aside to cool.

6. Add marinara sauce (1 tsp) over the baked zucchini bites.

7. Add the remaining mozzarella cheese over the marinara sauce to top.

8. Season with Italian seasoning and add the pepperoni mini slices.

9. Place the muffin pan under broiler to broil until the cheese is browned and melted, for 2 minutes to 3 minutes.

Nutritional Information/Serving

Calories 117 kcal, Dietary Fiber 1g, Net Carbs 3g, Protein 8g, Fat 8g

Keto Bacon Spinach Quiche (without Crust)

Preparation Time: 15 minutes

Cook Time: 45 minutes

Serves: 6 servings

Ingredients

Nutmeg (a pinch)

1/4 tsp pepper

3/4 tsp salt

8 oz (grated) cheddar cheese

3/4 cup heavy cream

1/4 medium (minced) onion

6 large eggs

16 oz bag (thawed & squeezed dry) frozen spinach

1/3 lb. (cooked until crispy & chopped) bacon

Directions

1. Heat up the oven to 350°F and grease a glass dish of 8 by 8".

2. In a big bowl, add nutmeg, pepper, salt, cheddar cheese, heavy cream, onion, eggs, chopped spinach and bacon.

3. Use a hand mixer to mix the spinach mixture together until it combines.

4. Transfer the spinach mixture into the greased glass dish and spread.

5. Transfer the glass dish into the center of the oven and bake for 40 minutes.

6. Serve the crustless spinach bacon quiche.

Nutritional Information/Serving

Calories 327 kcal, Protein 20g, Dietary Fiber 2.5g, Carbohydrates 6.5g, Fat 26g

Ketogenic Fathead Bagels

Preparation Time: 20 minutes

Cook Time: 20 minutes

Serves: 8 servings

Ingredients

2 large eggs

12 ounces mozzarella (pre-shredded part skim)

3/4 teaspoon xanthan gum

2 teaspoons baking powder

1/2 cup coconut flour

Topping

1 tablespoon (melted) butter

1/2 teaspoon coarse salt

1 teaspoon onion (dried minced)

1 teaspoon poppyseed

1 teaspoon sesame seeds

Directions

1. Use a silicone liner to line a baking pan and heat up the oven to 350°F.

2. Add xanthan gum, baking powder and coconut flour into a medium bowl and whisk.

3. Add the mozzarella cheese into a big microwaveable bowl and microwave until the cheese melts for 30 seconds on high.

4. Add eggs and the coconut flour mixture into the cheese bowl and use a spatula to mix the mixture.

5. On the lined baking pan, transfer the dough mixture and knead until solid.

6. Divide the dough into half. Divide each half into 4, making 8 pieces in total.

7. Roll each dough portions to form a dough log of 8" and lightly pinch the ends of the log together.

8. Add all the topping ingredient, except butter, into a flat-bottomed dish and stir.

9. Coat each dough log with the butter and dip each log into the mixed topping ingredients firmly.

10. On a silicone mat, add the doughs.

11. Place the baking pan into the oven and bake until bagels are golden, for 15 minutes to 20 minutes.

Nutritional Information/Serving

Calories 190 kcal, Protein 12.1g, Dietary Fiber 2.6g, Carbohydrates 5.5g, Fat 12.3g

Creamy Banana Muffin with Nuts

Preparation Time: 10 minutes

Cook Time: 20 minutes

Serves: 10 servings

Ingredients

1 tbsp powdered erythritol

1 tbsp almond flour

1 tbsp (cold & slice into 4 pieces) butter

3/4 cup walnuts, chopped

2 eggs

1/4 cup sour cream

1/4 cup almond milk, unsweetened

1 tsp vanilla extract

2 1/2 tsps banana extract

5 tbsps melted, butter

1/2 tsps cinnamon, ground

2 tsps baking powder

1/2 cup powdered erythritol

1 ¼ cup almond flour

Directions

1. Line muffin tin with 10 paper liners, let sit and heat up the oven to 350°F.

2. Add cinnamon, baking powder, erythritol and almond flour into a big bowl. Stir the mixture together.

3. Add in sour cream, almond milk, vanilla extract, banana extract and butter into the almond flour bowl.

4. Stir the mixture and add egg. Lightly stir mixture to combine.

5. Scoop the batter into the prepared muffin tin, 1/2 to 3/4 of each cup.

6. In a food processor, add almond flour, butter and walnuts. Process the nuts into smaller pieces.

Note: Add a tbsp of butter if the mixture is really dry.

7. Over the batter in each muffin cup, evenly sprinkle with the walnut mixture and use a spoon to gently press in the walnut mixture.

8. Add erythritol to the mixture in the pan.

9. Transfer the muffin tin into the oven and bake until the batter is brown for 20 minutes.

10. Set aside to cool for 1 hour to firm up.

Nutritional Information/Serving

Calories 248 kcal, Fat 22g, Protein 7g, Net Carbs 4g, Dietary Fiber 3g

Rosemary Cauliflower Bread

Preparation Time: 15 minutes

Cook Time: 45 minutes

Serves: 18 servings

Ingredients

1 tablespoon (chopped) fresh parsley

1 tablespoon (chopped) fresh rosemary

6 cloves (minced) garlic

6 tablespoons ghee

1 teaspoon sea salt

1 1/2 tablespoons baking powder

1 1/4 cup coconut flour

1/4 teaspoon cream of tartar

10 large (separate the whites and yolks) egg

3 cups cauliflower rice

Directions

1. Use parchment paper to line a 5 by 9" loaf pan and heat up the oven to 350°F.

2. Add the cauliflower rice into a microwaveable bowl and cover it.

3. Place the cauliflower rice bowl into the microwave.

4. Cook the cauliflower rice until it is tender for 3 minutes to 4 minutes. Set aside to cool.

5. In a bowl, add the cream of tartar and egg whites.

6. Whisk the egg-whites mixture together with a hand mixer.

7. In a food processor, add 1/4 of whisked egg whites, minced garlic, butter, egg yolks, salt, baking powder and coconut flour.

8. On a kitchen towel, transfer the cooked cauliflower, squeeze to release liquid until it becomes clumped together and dry.

9. In the food processor with the coconut flour, add the squeezed cauliflower and process until it is lightly crumbled and solid.

10. Gently add in the remaining egg-whites mixture into the food processor and process in short bursts.

Note: The mixture will become fluffy.

11. Add in the rosemary and the parsley. Mix lightly.

12. On the prepared baking pan, transfer the batter and use a spatula to gently smooth the upper part and around it.

13. Transfer the pan into the oven and bake until the top is brown for 45 minutes to 50 minutes.

14. Set aside to completely cool before slicing.

Nutritional Information/Serving

Calories 108 kcal, Dietary Fiber 5g, Net Carbs 3g, Protein 6g, Fat 8g

Simple and Tasty Egg Muffins

Preparation Time: 20 minutes

Cook Time: 20 minutes

Serves: 12 servings

Ingredients

¼ Cup coconut Milk

¾ teaspoon salt

Ground Pepper

9 eggs

1 teaspoon (chopped) fresh oregano

1 1/2 Cups (packed) fresh spinach

¾ Cup (thinly sliced) red bell Peppers

½ Sweet (thinly sliced) onion

1 tablespoon olive oil

8 ounces pork breakfast sausage

Directions

1. Grease a muffin tin and heat up the oven to 350°F.

2. At med-high heat, place a skillet over heat and add in the breakfast sausage.

3. Use a spoon to break the sausage into pieces while cooking.

4. Add in fresh oregano, peppers, onion and olive oil when the sausage is halfway cooked.

5. Cook the sausage mixture until the onions becomes translucent.

6. Add in fresh spinach and use a lid to cover the skillet.

7. Saute sausage mixture until the spinach wilts for 30 seconds, take the lid off and toss the mixture together.

8. Take the skillet off heat.

9. Add coconut milk, salt and eggs into a big bowl.

10. Whisk the egg mixture until the eggs are beaten.

11. Stir in the veggies and sausage into the egg mixture bowl. Stir together until it is combined.

12. Share the veggie-egg mixture into the prepared muffin tins.

13. Transfer the muffin tin into the oven and bake for 18 minutes to 20 minutes.

14. Set aside the muffin tin, for a few minutes.

15. Use a knife to loosen the ends of the muffins to make removal easy.

Nutritional Information/Serving

Calories 143 kcal, Protein 10.4g, Sugars 1.3g, Dietary Fiber 1.6g, Carbohydrate 4g, Total Fat 9.8g

Peppered Cheese Keto Pizza (Breakfast)
Preparation Time: 10 minutes

Cook Time: 30 minutes

Serves: 8 servings

Ingredients

1 cup (shredded) cheese

2 cups (sliced) peppers

8 ounces sausage

1/4 tsp pepper

1/2 tsp salt

1/2 cup heavy cream

12 eggs

Directions

1. Heat up the oven to 350°F.

2. In a microwaveable bowl, add sliced peppers and microwave for about 3 minutes.

3. Add sausage into a heavy bottomed skillet, cook the sausage until brown and transfer into a bowl. Let stand.

4. In another skillet, add in pepper, salt, heavy cream and eggs.

5. Mix together and cook until the sides are just solid, for 5 minutes.

6. Transfer the egg mixture into the oven and bake for 15 minutes.

7. Add in the cheese, cooked sliced pepper and sausage into the baked egg.

8. Set oven to broiler and broil pizza for 3 minutes. Set aside for 5 minutes to cool.

Nutritional Information/Serving

Calories 307 kcal, Net Carbs 2.1g, Protein 18.4g, Dietary Fiber 0.5g, Fat 24.3g

LUNCH

Keto Cauliflower Egg Salad

Preparation Time: 5 minutes

Cook Time: 10 minutes

Serves: 5 servings

Ingredients

2 large (hard boiled and chopped) eggs

1/3 cup (finely diced) celery

1/3 cup (finely diced) onion

1/4 teaspoon black pepper

1/2 teaspoon sea salt

1/2 teaspoon paprika

1/2 teaspoon garlic powder

1 tablespoon Dijon mustard

1 tablespoon apple cider vinegar

2/3 cup mayo

1 large (cut into small florets) cauliflower head

Directions

1. In a big bowl, add 2 tbsps of water and cauliflower florets.

2. Place the cauliflower bowl into the microwave and cook for 10 minutes on high.

3. Stir the cauliflower after the first 5 minutes and drain the moisture.

4. In a bowl, add black pepper, salt, paprika, garlic powder, dijon mustard, vinegar and mayo.

5. Whisk together until a fine texture is formed.

6. Add the egg, diced celery, diced onion and the drained cauliflower into the dressing mixture in the bowl and stir together.

7. Garnish with more paprika if needed.

Nutritional Information/Serving

Calories 250 kcal, Dietary Fiber 5g, Net Carbs 6g, Fat 21g

Keto Hamburger Buns
Preparation Time: 10 minutes

Cook Time: 25 minutes

Serves: 12 servings

Ingredients

1/4 cup coconut oil

1/2 cup avocado oil

2 large eggs

2 cups egg whites

3/4 teaspoon sea salt

1 1/2 teaspoons baking soda

1 cup coconut flour

3/4 cup water (warm)

6 tablespoons whole psyllium husks

Directions

1. Grease a muffin pan lightly and heat up the oven to 350°F.

2. In a small bowl, add water and psyllium husks.

3. Mix together and let stand until it thickens to a gel texture.

4. In a food processor, add coconut oil, avocado oil, eggs, egg whites, salt, baking soda and coconut flour.

5. Pulse the egg-white mixture until it evenly combines.

6. Stir in the psyllium gel into the egg-white mixture in the food processor and process until combined.

7. Evenly share the batter among the prepared muffin cups and use hands to smoothen the top.

8. Transfer the muffin pan into the oven and bake until the ends are golden, for 25 minutes to 30 minutes.

Note: Check for doneness by inserting a toothpick.

9. Set aside muffins, for 10 minutes to 15 minutes to cool.

10. Transfer the buns onto a rack to cool completely.

Nutritional Information/Serving

Calories 198 kcal, Dietary Fiber 6g, Net Carbs 2g, Protein 8g, Fat 17g

Keto Turkey Burgers

Preparation Time: 15 minutes

Cook Time: 15 minutes

Serves: 4 servings

Ingredients (Mexican turkey burgers)

1 tbsp olive oil

1/2 tsp salt

1 tbsp lime juice

2 cloves (minced) garlic

2 green (finely sliced) onions

1/4 cup cilantro (finely chopped)

1/3 cup red bell pepper (finely chopped)

1 lb. turkey (ground)

Topping

Jalapenos (sliced)

Tomatoes (sliced)

White onions (sliced)

Guacamole

Romaine lettuce

Directions

1. Heat up indoor grill pan to med-high heat and rub olive oil on the grill pan.

2. Add salt, lime juice, minced garlic, green onions, chopped cilantro, red bell pepper and turkey into a medium mixing bowl.

3. Mix together with a fork. Divide into 4 equal round patties.

4. Season each patty with a pinch of salt and dribble olive oil over the patties.

5. Transfer the patties onto the preheated grill and grill each side until 165°F internal temperature is reached, for 5 minutes to 8 minutes.

6. Take the burgers off heat and set aside for 5 minutes to cool.

7. Serve burgers warm on romaine lettuce. Top burgers with sliced jalapenos, guacamole, tomatoes and white onions.

Nutritional Information/Serving

Calories 205 kcal, Protein 22.7g, Carbs 1.5g, Fat 12.1g

Keto Tuna Salad

Preparation Time: 10 minutes

Cook Time: 0 minutes

Serves: 8 servings

Ingredients

1/8 teaspoon black pepper

1/2 cup walnuts, toasted (chopped)

1/2 teaspoon lemon juice (fresh)

1 cup mayo

1 avocado (seeded, peeled and diced)

1 medium (diced and seeded) granny smith apple

1 medium onion (finely diced)

4 (5-ounces) tuna in water (well drained)

Directions

1. In a big mixing bowl, add lemon juice, black pepper (a pinch), chopped walnuts, mayo, avocado, granny smith apple, onion and water.

2. Stir to combine salad mixture. Serve.

Nutritional Information/Serving

Calories 360 kcal, Iron 1.7mg, Calcium 45mg, Protein 16g, Sugar 3g, Dietary Fiber 3g, Carbohydrates 8g, Fat 29g

Mexican Beef Taco Salad

Preparation Time: 10 minutes

Cook Time: 10 minutes

Serves: 6 servings

Ingredients

1/3 cup sour cream

1/3 cup salsa

1/2 cup (chopped) green onions

1 medium (cubed) avocado

1 1/3 cups (halved) grape tomatoes

8 ounces (chopped) Romaine lettuce

2 tablespoons taco seasoning

1 teaspoon olive oil

1 pound beef (ground)

Directions

1. On high heat, place a saute pan over heat and add in olive oil.

2. Add in beef and stir-fry until the moisture is dried and the ground beef is browned, for 7 minutes to 10 minutes.

3. Use a spatula to break the ground beef into pieces.

4. Season the beef with taco seasoning and stir until it combines.

5. In a big bowl, add in sour cream, salsa, green onions, avocado, grape tomatoes and romaine lettuce.

6. Add in the cooked ground beef into the romaine lettuce bowl.

7. Toss the mixture together. Serve.

Nutritional Information/Serving

Calories 332 kcal, Sugar 2g, Dietary Fiber 4g, Net Carbs 5g, Total Carbs 9g, Protein 20g, Fat 25g

Tzatziki Sauced Meatballs (Keto Mediterranean)

Preparation Time: 20 minutes

Cook Time: 12 minutes

Serves: 4 servings

Ingredients (Greek meatballs)

2 oz (crumbled) feta cheese

Fresh black pepper (ground)

Kosher salt

1/4 tsp cinnamon (ground)

1/2 tsp cumin (ground)

1/2 tsp coriander (ground)

1 tsp oregano (dried)

1 egg

2 tbsps fresh lemon juice

Lemon zest

1 clove (grated) garlic

3 tbsps onion (grated)

1/4 cup fresh parsley leaf (chopped)

1/4 cup breadcrumbs

1 lb. lean beef (ground)

Sauce

Fresh black pepper (ground)

Kosher salt

1/2 tsp garlic (grated)

1 tbsp fresh dill (chopped)

Lemon juice (half of a lemon)

1 1/2 cups Greek yogurt, plain non-fat

1 cup cucumber (shredded)

Directions

1. Use foil to line a baking pan and grease with cooking spray. Heat up the oven to 450°F.

2. Add pepper, kosher salt, spices, egg, grated garlic, onion, chopped parsley, feta cheese and breadcrumbs into a big bowl. Whisk together.

3. Add in beef into the feta cheese bowl. Use hands to lightly mix until combined.

4. Form a meatball with a tbsp of the beef mixture, repeat with the remaining beef mixture.

5. Arrange the meatballs on the lined baking pan and spray the top of meatballs with cooking spray.

6. Transfer the baking pan onto the middle rack of the oven.

7. Bake until the meatballs are golden brown, for 12 minutes to 15 minutes.

8. In a medium bowl, add in black pepper, salt, garlic, dill, lemon juice, yogurt and cucumber.

9. Whisk the sauce mixture until it combines.

10. Take out the baked meatballs from the oven and serve with sauce.

Nutritional Information/Serving

Calories 400 kcal, Protein 42g, Dietary Fiber 2g, Carbohydrates 22g, Saturated Fat 6g, Total Fat 16g

Buttery Crab Filled Salmon

Preparation Time: 10 minutes

Cook Time: 25 minutes

Serves: 8 servings

Ingredients (salmon)

Toothpicks

Black pepper

Sea salt

2 tablespoons (melted) butter

2 tablespoons lemon zest

2 pounds (cut into wider fillet) salmon

Filling

1 teaspoon old bay seasoning

1 tablespoon lemon juice

2 cloves (minced) garlic

2 tablespoons (chopped) fresh parsley

2 tablespoons mayo

1/2 large (chopped) onion

8 ounces lump crab meat

Directions

1. Use foil to line a baking pan and heat up the oven to 400°F.

2. At med-heat, place a skillet over heat and add in the chopped onion.

3. Cook until the onion is golden and translucent, for 7 minutes to 10 minutes.

4. In a bowl, add the old bay seasoning, lemon juice, chopped parsley, garlic and mayo. Whisk together.

5. Add the cooked onion into the mayo mixture bowl and stir together.

6. Fold crab meat into the mayo mixture gently. The lumps should not break apart.

7. On the lined baking pan, add the salmon fillets

8. Add the crab mixture on the fish fillets.

9. Begin from the thinner end of the fish fillet and fold over filling to the wider end.

10. In a bowl, add lemon zest and butter. Whisk together.

11. Brush the salmon top with the lemon zest mixture.

12. Lightly season salmon with black pepper and salt.

13. Transfer the baking pan into the oven and bake until fish fillet is easily flaked with a fork, for 16 minutes to 20 minutes.

14. Sprinkle more chopped parsley over the salmon and cut each fillet cross-wise before serving.

Nutritional Information/Serving

Calories 243 kcal, Dietary Fiber 0.2g, Net Carbs 0.8g, Protein 29g, Fat 13g

Keto Crack Slaw with Pork

Preparation Time: 5 minutes

Cook Time: 25 minutes

Serves: 4 servings

Ingredients

2 tbsps sesame seeds (toasted)

1 tbsp rice vinegar

3 tbsps soy sauce

14 oz bag coleslaw mix

1 tbsp garlic chili sauce

Black pepper

Sea salt

1/2 tsp ginger (ground)

1 lb. pork (ground)

5 green onions (sliced green & white part separately)

1/2 cup (diced) onion

3 cloves (minced) garlic

2 tbsps sesame oil

Directions

1. On med-high heat, place a big pan and add in 2 tablespoons of sesame oil.

2. Add in green onion (white part only), diced onion and minced garlic into the heated sesame oil in the pan.

3. Mix the onion mixture together and saute until the garlic is aromatic and onions becomes translucent.

4. Add in garlic chili sauce, black pepper, salt, ginger and pork into the pan.

5. Saute the ground pork mixture until is well cooked.

6. Add in rice vinegar, soy sauce and coleslaw mix into the ground pork mixture in the pan.

7. Cook the ground pork mixture until coleslaw mix becomes soft.

8. Garnish with toasted sesame seeds, green onion (the green part) and serve.

Nutritional Information/Serving

Calories 297 kcal, Net Carbs 5.5g, Dietary Fiber 1.5g, Protein 20g, Fat 20g

Keto Spinach Filled Salmon Bake

Preparation Time: 10 minutes

Cook Time: 15 minutes

Serves: 4 servings

Ingredients (salmon)

1 tbsp butter, unsalted

2 tbsps olive oil

2 tbsps lemon juice

Pepper

Salt

4 salmon fillets (skinless), slit 3/4 quarter of the fillet

Filling

1 tbsp lemon juice

1 tbsp garlic (minced)

1 tbsp butter (unsalted)

Pepper

Salt

2 tsps garlic (minced)

1/4 cup parmesan cheese (finely grated)

4 ounces spinach thawed (frozen)

4 ounces (room temperature) cream cheese

Directions

1. Lay the skinless fish fillets on a plain work surface.

2. Add lemon juice, olive oil (one tbsp), pepper and salt on both sides of the fillets to season.

3. Squeeze the thawed spinach to remove excess liquid.

4. Add minced garlic, grated parmesan cheese, cream cheese and the squeezed spinach into a med-size bowl.

5. Mix together and sprinkle pepper and salt over the cream cheese/spinach mixture to season.

6. Add a tbsp to 2 tbsps of spinach mixture into the slit/pocket of each fillet and spread.

7. Grease a baking sheet lightly and heat up the oven to 350°F.

8. Transfer the stuffed fish fillet onto the prepared baking sheet.

9. Transfer the baking sheet into the oven.

10. Bake until the fillet flakes easy with a fork, is opaque in the middle and is well cooked, for 10 minutes to 15 minutes.

11. Transfer the juice in the baking sheet into a pan and add in a tablespoon of lemon juice, garlic and unsalted butter.

12. Mix the lemon juice together and cook for 30 seconds, until the garlic is aromatic.

13. Serve the spinach filled salmon with the cooked lemon juice mixture.

Nutritional Information/Serving

Calories 428 kcal, Protein 41g, Carbohydrates 9g, Fat 24g

Filled Pepper Lasagna

Preparation Time: 15 minutes

Cook Time: 1 hour

Serves: 6 servings

Ingredients

Black pepper

Sea salt

1 cup (shredded) mozzarella cheese

1 cup ricotta cheese

1 tablespoon Italian seasoning

2 cups homemade marinara

4 cloves (minced) garlic

1 1/2 pound beef (ground)

6 large bell pepper

Directions

1. On med-high heat, place a skillet over heat and add the minced garlic.

2. Saute the garlic until it is aromatic, for 30 seconds.

3. Add in the beef and saute for 10 minutes until the beef is golden. Use a spatula to break the beef apart while cooking.

4. Add in the salt, black pepper, Italian seasoning and marinara sauce.

5. Stir and simmer the sauce mixture on low heat, for 10 minutes.

6. Use a silicone mat to line a baking pan and heat up the oven to 375°F.

7. Cut the top of the 6 bell peppers, remove the ribs and seeds of the pepper.

8. Gently cut the base of the pepper in a very tin slit.

9. In each bell pepper, stuff it with 1 tbsp to 2 tbsps of meat sauce, mozzarella cheese and ricotta cheese.

10. Repeat the above method until each bell pepper is filled.

11. Transfer the stuffed peppers onto the prepared baking pan and tent the peppers with aluminum foil.

Note: The aluminum foil shouldn't rest on the cheese in the stuffed peppers.

12. Transfer the baking pan into the oven and bake for about 30 minutes.

13. Open the oven, remove the aluminum foil and bake the stuffed pepper until the cheeses are golden and melts, for 10 minutes.

Nutritional Information/Serving

Calories 412 kcal, Dietary Fiber 2g, Net Carbs 8g, Protein 30g, Fat 27g

Filled Keto Tortillas with Spicy Sauce

Preparation Time: 20 minutes

Cook Time: 20 minutes

Serves: 6 servings

Ingredients

Cayenne pepper

1/2 teaspoon garlic powder

3/4 teaspoon paprika

2 tablespoons jar jalapenos in water (minced and include the liquid)

6 tablespoons mayo

Cauliflower wraps

1/2 teaspoon xanthan gum

1/2 teaspoon sea salt

3/4 cup (shredded) mozzarella cheese

3 large egg

1 1/2 pounds (cut into florets) cauliflower

Filling

1 1/2 cups (shredded) cheddar cheese

Directions

1. Use parchment paper to line a baking pan and heat up the oven to 400°F.

2. In a food processor, add cauliflower florets and pulse until a rice texture is formed.

3. Move the cauliflower rice into a big bowl.

4. Microwave cauliflower rice until it is cooked through, for 8 minutes to 10 minutes on high.

5. Set aside the cooked cauliflower rice to cool.

6. On a cheese towel, transfer the cauliflower and get rid of the moisture by squeezing the cheese towel.

Note: The cauliflower rice will become clumpy and dense after squeezing the liquid.

7. Return the cauliflower rice into the food processor and change to S blade.

8. Add in sea salt, mozzarella cheese and eggs into the food processor and process until a fine texture is formed.

9. On the cauliflower mixture, sprinkle xanthan gum and process until combined.

10. On the prepared baking pan, divide the mixture into 6 portions and spread each portion into a thin circle with a spatula.

11. Transfer the baking pan into the oven and bake until the base is brown and ends are dry, for 8 minutes to 10 minutes.

12. Turn each tortilla over and bake again for 4 minutes to 6 minutes on the second side.

13. Leave the baking pan in the oven to cool, for about 10 minutes before removing.

14. In a small airtight container, add cayenne pepper, garlic powder, paprika, jalapenos and mayo. Whisk together.

15. Cover the container and place in the refrigerator.

16. On each tortilla, add 1 tbsp of the sauce and spread, sprinkle cheddar cheese about 1/4 cup and fold each tortilla.

17. At med-heat, place an oiled skillet over heat and arrange 2 tortillas into the heated skillet.

18. Fry until it is golden for a couple of minutes. Turn and fry other side for a couple of minutes.

19. Repeat the process above with the remaining wrap and sauce.

Nutritional Information/Serving

Calories 108 kcal, Dietary Fiber 3g, Net Carbs 4g, Protein 9g, Fat 5g

Keto Jalapeno Cornbread Muffins
Preparation Time: 10 minutes

Cook Time: 20 minutes

Serves: 8 servings

Ingredients

7 ounces can jalapenos slices (drained and finely chopped)

1/4 cup coconut milk beverage (unsweetened)

1/3 cup (measured solid and melted) coconut oil

5 large (at room temperature) eggs

3/4 teaspoon sea salt

2 teaspoons baking powder

3 tablespoons erythritol

2/3 cup coconut flour

Directions

1. Use parchment liners to line 8 muffin cups, and heat up the oven to 350°F.

2. Add salt, baking powder, erythritol and coconut flour into a big bowl and stir together.

3. In another bowl, add in the jalapenos, coconut oil, coconut milk and eggs.

4. Mix the egg mixture together and stir into the coconut flour mixture.

5. Stir together until it is combined.

6. Share the batter among the lined 8 muffin cups and transfer into the oven.

7. Bake until the upper part is springy, and an inserted toothpick comes out clean, for 18 minutes to 22 minutes.

Nutritional Information/Serving

Calories 154 kcal, Dietary Fiber 5g, Net Carbs 3g, Protein 7g, Fat 13g

Keto Coleslaw Recipe

Preparation Time: 5 minutes

Cook Time: 0 minutes

Serves: 6 servings

Ingredients

Black pepper

Sea salt

1 teaspoon celery seed

1 tablespoon erythritol (powdered)

2 tablespoons apple cider vinegar

1/4 cup mayo

4 cups coleslaw mix (shredded)

Directions

1. In a big bowl, add in the coleslaw mix and let stand.

2. Add celery, powdered erythritol, apple cider vinegar and mayo into a small bowl. Whisk all together.

3. Sprinkle black pepper and salt over the mayo mixture to season.

4. Stir mayo mixture into the coleslaw bowl.

5. Toss the mixture to coat evenly.

6. Transfer the coleslaw into the fridge to develop the flavors, for 1 hour.

7. Stir and serve the coleslaw chilled.

Nutritional Information/Serving

Calories 87 kcal, Dietary Fiber 2g, Net Carbs 2g, Protein 1g, Fat 8g

Almond Flour Meatloaf

Preparation Time: 10 minutes

Cook Time: 1 hour

Serves: 12 servings

Ingredients

1/3 cup ketchup

1/2 teaspoon black pepper

2 teaspoons sea salt

1 tablespoon Italian seasoning

2 large eggs

2 tablespoons coconut aminos

3 ounces tomato paste

8 cloves (minced) garlic

1/2 large (diced) onion

1/2 cup almond flour

2 pounds beef (ground)

Directions

1. Grease a loaf pan of 5 by 9", and heat up the oven to 350°F. Let the pan stand.

2. Add black pepper, salt, Italian seasoning, eggs, coconut aminos, tomato paste, garlic, onion, almond flour and ground beef into a big bowl.

3. Mix ground beef mixture together, until it is lightly combined.

4. Move the ground beef mixture into the greased loaf pan and place into the oven.

5. Bake the mixture for 30 minutes.

6. Top the meatloaf with ketchup and spread.

7. Return the loaf pan into the oven and bake until meatloaf is well cooked, for 25 minutes to 45 minutes.

8. Set aside to cool for 10 minutes and use a knife to slice the meatloaf.

Nutritional Information/Serving

Calories 215 kcal, Dietary Fiber 2g, Net Carbs 3g, Protein 17g, Fat 14g

Fried Cauliflower Rice with Steak

Preparation Time: 15 minutes

Cook Time: 15 minutes

Serves: 3 servings

Ingredients (steak)

2 large fried eggs

1 pound (remove silver skin) skirt steak, score in a small criss-crosscut pattern with a sharp knife

Cauliflower Fried Rice

Avocado oil

Coarse salt

1 teaspoon sesame oil

2 teaspoons coconut aminos

¼ teaspoon (grated) ginger

2 small (finely chopped) garlic cloves

2-3 bulbs (chopped) scallions, separate green and white parts

2 cups cauliflower rice

Steak seasonings

Black pepper

2 large (crushed) garlic cloves

Quarter of one whole lime juice

½ teaspoon coarse salt

3 tablespoons coconut aminos

Tomato sauce

Lime juice

2 tablespoons (finely chopped) flat parsley

1 ½ tablespoons (finely chopped) shallots

1 medium (finely chopped) ripe tomato,

Directions

1. In a bowl, add the skirt steak, black pepper, garlic, lime juice, coarse salt and coconut aminos.

2. Mix together to coat the steak. Place the steak bowl into a refrigerator to marinate, for an hour to 2 hours.

3. Remove the steak bowl from the refrigerator and shake off excess marinade.

4. Place a heavy bottom skillet over heat, add in ghee (a tablespoon) and the marinated steak.

5. Saute each side of the steak for 2 minutes to 3 minutes or until desired doneness is reached.

6. On high-heat, place a pan over heat and add in avocado oil.

7. Reduce the heat to low-heat, add in garlic and scallions (white parts only) into the pan with the avocado oil.

8. Sprinkle a pinch of coarse salt over the scallion mixture, and saute for 10 seconds, until the garlic is aromatic.

9. Add in sesame oil, coconut aminos, ginger and cauliflower rice into the pan with the scallion mixture.

10. Sprinkle a pinch of salt over the cauliflower mixture in the pan, and stir-cook until the cauliflower rice becomes tender.

11. Put off the heat and take pan off heat.

12. Add in scallion (green parts) to the pan and stir together.

13. Serve sliced steak against the grain, with tomato sauce, fried eggs and cauliflower rice.

Nutritional Information/Serving

Calories 341 kcal, Dietary Fiber 2g, Fat 17.5g, Protein 39g, Carbohydrates 8g

Delicious Baked Peri Peri Chicken

Preparation Time: 15 minutes

Cook Time: 1 hour

Serves: 4 servings

Ingredients

Black pepper

½ tsp salt

1 medium lemon (juice only)

1 tsp paprika (smoked)

½ cup coconut milk

¼ cup olive oil

¼ cup onions (chopped)

1-2 tbsps oregano (fresh)

4 large basil leaves

3-4 garlic cloves

1 fresh chili pepper (chopped roughly)

1 fresh jalapeno peppers (seeds removed & chopped roughly)

¼ medium red pepper

Pepper

Salt

3 1/2 – 4 lbs. (cut up) chicken

Directions

1. In a food processor, add in the chopped onions, fresh oregano, basil, garlic cloves, chopped chili pepper, chopped jalapenos pepper and red pepper.

2. Process the onion mixture and add in coconut milk and olive oil into the food processor.

3. Process the coconut milk mixture and add in black pepper, lemon juice and smoked paprika into the food processor.

4. Mix and transfer the coconut mixture into a bowl. Season with salt and place the coconut milk bowl into the fridge.

5. Remove the chicken excess fat by trimming and transfer on a paper napkin to pat dry.

6. Rub the chicken with lemon juice. Sprinkle the chicken with pepper and salt to season.

7. Immerse the trimmed chicken into the refrigerated coconut milk mixture until completely coated.

8. Transfer the chicken into a zip lock bag. Place the zip lock bag into a fridge for 2 hours.

9. Take chicken from the zip lock bag with a thong and return the marinade into the fridge.

10. Shake off the excess marinade from the chicken.

11. Use a foil to line a baking sheet and place a wire rack on the foil. Heat up a oven to 425°F.

12. On the prepared baking sheet, add the marinated chicken pieces and arrange in a layer.

13. Place the baking sheet into the oven.

14. Bake chicken for 45 minutes to 50 minutes, until the chicken skin is crisped and chicken is well cooked.

Note: Rotate the chicken after the first 20 minutes of baking.

15. Transfer the lemon juice mixture and the remaining marinade into a small saucepan.

16. Simmer for 7 minutes and serve with the baked chicken.

Nutritional Information/Serving

Calories 240 kcal, Protein 105g, Dietary Fiber 1g, Carbohydrates 5g, Fat 104g

Cauliflower Chicken Bake

Preparation Time: 5 minutes

Cook Time: 25 minutes

Serves: 8 servings

Ingredients

Fresh (cut into ribbons) basil

Black pepper

Sea salt

1 cup (shredded) mozzarella cheese

1/4 cup coconut cream

3/4 cup basil pesto

1 pound (cooked and packed tightly to measure) chicken, shredded

1 tablespoon olive oil

1 head (cut into florets) cauliflower

Directions

1. Use parchment paper to line a casserole dish of 13 by 9", and heat up the oven to 400°F.

2. Add olive oil and cauliflower into the prepared dish and toss to coat.

3. Lightly season the cauliflower with black pepper and salt.

4. Transfer the dish into the oven and bake until it is soft and crispy, for 15 minutes to 20 minutes.

5. Reduce the oven heat to 350°F.

6. Add 1/2 cup of mozzarella cheese and chicken into the casserole dish. Mix together.

7. Add coconut cream and basil pesto into a bowl and stir together.

8. Stir in the basil pesto mixture into the dish and mix until the chicken mixture is evenly coated.

9. Sprinkle the remaining 1/2 cup of mozzarella cheese over the chicken mixture, to top.

10. Place back the dish into the oven and bake until the cheese releases bubbles and is melted, for 10 minutes to 15 minutes.

11. Add the fresh basil to garnish.

Nutritional Information/Serving

Calories 270 kcal, Dietary Fiber 4g, Net Carbs 6g, Protein 16g, Fat 19g

Tasty Bacon Chicken Casserole

Preparation Time: 5 minutes

Cook Time: 15 minutes

Serves: 8 servings

Ingredients

Water

4 cups (cut into florets) broccoli

1 cup (shredded and divided) cheddar cheese

1 cup (shredded and divided) mozzarella cheese

3/4 cup ranch dressing

3 cloves (minced) garlic

8 slices (cooked and chopped) bacon

2 pounds (cooked and shredded) chicken breast

Directions

1. Heat up the oven to 375°F.

2. In a pot, add water and the broccoli. Boil the broccoli florets.

3. Reduce to simmer and simmer the broccoli until it is bright green for a minute to 2 minutes.

4. In a big bowl, add half of cheddar cheese, half of mozzarella cheese, ranch dressing, minced garlic, cooked broccoli, chopped bacon and chicken breast.

5. Stir the chicken breast mixture until combined.

6. In a glass casserole dish of 13 by 9", transfer the chicken breast mixture.

7. Add the cheddar cheese and the remaining mozzarella cheese to top the chicken breast mixture.

8. Transfer the dish into the oven, bake until casserole releases bubbles and is hot, for 15 minutes.

Nutritional Information/Serving

Calories 469 kcal, Dietary Fiber 2g, Net Carbs 5g, Protein 38g, Fat 31g

Keto Chicken Bacon Shells

Preparation Time: 10 minutes

Cook Time: 15 minutes

Serves: 4 servings

Ingredients

1/4 teaspoon sea salt

2 cloves (minced) garlic

1 1/2 cup (cooked) bacon bits

1/4 cup mayo

4 large chicken breasts

Directions

1. Grease foil lightly and line a baking pan with the greased foil. Heat up the oven to 450°F.

2. Add salt, minced garlic and cooked bacon bits into a blender. Pulse the bacon bits mixture until the bacon is crumbled into smaller pieces.

3. In a big bowl, transfer the crumbled bacon bits.

4. In a medium bowl, add in the mayo and coat each chicken breast until thin layer cover is reached, by dipping into the mayo.

5. Add each coated chicken breast into the bowl with bacon bits and roll to coat all parts.

6. Transfer the coated chicken breast onto the prepared baking pan.

7. Transfer the baking pan into the oven and bake until the bacon is crisped and the chicken is well cooked, for 15 minutes to 18 minutes.

Nutritional Information/Serving

Calories 606 kcal, Dietary Fiber 0.1g, Net Carbs 0.4g, Protein 45g, Fat 43g

Cheese Chicken Caesar Salad

Preparation Time: 10 minutes

Cook Time: 6 minutes

Serves: 8 servings

Ingredients (salad)

2 large (grilled and sliced) chicken breasts

8 ounces (shredded) parmesan cheese

2 cup (halved) grape tomatoes

1 head (chopped) romaine lettuce

Dressing

Black pepper

Sea salt

1 clove (minced) garlic

1 teaspoon Worcestershire sauce

1 teaspoon anchovy paste

1 teaspoon lemon juice

1 tablespoon olive oil

3 tablespoons mayo

Directions

1. Add black pepper, salt, Worcestershire sauce, anchovy paste, lemon juice, olive oil and mayo into a bowl.

2. Whisk until a fine texture is formed.

Note: If the dressing is too thick, add more olive oil to thin out as needed.

3. Cover the bowl with the dressing mixture and place in the fridge.

4. Use parchment paper to line a baking pan and heat up the oven to 400°F.

5. On the prepared baking pan, add the shredded parmesan cheese in tbsp-size circles and leave 2" space.

6. Transfer the baking pan into the oven. Bake until cheese becomes brown at the ends and melts for 6 minutes to 8 minutes.

7. Set aside the cheese to cool until it is crisped in the baking pan.

8. In a bowl, add the cooked chicken, grape tomatoes and Romaine lettuce. Toss together to combine.

9. Crumble the baked parmesan cheese into smaller pieces with your hands and add into the bowl with the salad.

10. Dribble the mayo mixture over the salad and toss to coat.

Nutritional Information/Serving

Calories 184 kcal, Dietary Fiber 2g, Net Carbs 3g, Protein 11g, Fat 13g

Chicken Breast Bake

Preparation Time: 15 minutes

Cook Time: 15 minutes

Serves: 4 servings

Ingredients

Black pepper

Sea salt

2 teaspoons garlic powder

4 teaspoons Italian seasoning

4 teaspoons olive oil

2 tablespoons sea salt

4 large chicken breasts

Directions

1. Add water into a big bowl, add in salt and mix until salt is almost completely dissolved.

2. Add the chicken breasts into the water with salt and set aside for 10 minutes to brine the chicken breasts.

Note: The water should cover the chicken breasts.

3. Use parchment paper to line a baking sheet, and grease. Heat up the oven to 450°F.

4. Pat to dry the brined chicken breasts and lay on the prepared baking pan.

5. Use olive oil to brush each chicken breast and season with black pepper, salt, 1/4 teaspoon of garlic powder, and 1/2 teaspoon of Italian seasoning.

6. Turn the chicken breasts and repeat the above seasoning process on the other side.

7. Transfer the baking pan into the oven and bake until the chicken is not pink in color, for 15 minutes to 18 minutes.

Nutritional Information/Serving

Calories 226 kcal, Dietary Fiber 0.2g, Net Carbs 1.8g, Protein 27g, Fat 12g

Zoodle Chicken Keto Caprese

Preparation Time: 10 minutes

Cook Time: 20 minutes

Serves: 2 servings

Ingredients

2 ounces (cut in half) fresh mini mozzarella balls

1 (spiralized with blade D) large zucchini

1 tablespoon fresh basil, chopped

Ground black pepper

Kosher Salt

A pinch crushed red pepper flakes

3/4 pound grape tomatoes, divide into half

3 chopped, garlic cloves

1 tbsp olive oil

1/4 tsp dried oregano

kosher salt

1/2 pound boneless skinless chicken breast (slice into 1/2" cubes)

Directions

1. In a medium bowl, add the chicken breast. Sprinkle dried oregano, black pepper and salt (1/2 tsp) over the chicken to season.

2. At med-heat, place a big non-stick skillet over heat and add olive oil (1/2 tbsp).

3. Transfer the seasoned chicken into the skillet and stir-cook for 6 minutes until well cooked and golden.

4. Move chicken into a bowl and let stand.

5. Add chopped garlic cloves and 1/2 tbsp of olive oil into the skillet.

6. Saute for 30 seconds over med-heat until the garlic becomes brown.

7. Add black pepper, salt (1/4 tsp), pepper flakes and tomatoes into the skillet.

8. Place lid over skillet. At low-heat, simmer mixture for 15 minutes until tomatoes becomes tender.

9. Add the remaining salt, chopped basil and the spiralized zucchini into the skillet.

10. Stir-cook for 2 minutes at high-heat.

11. Add mozzarella balls and return the cooked chicken into the skillet.

12. Serve.

Nutritional Information/Serving

Calories 342 kcal, Dietary Fiber 4g, Fat 17g, Protein 34g, Carbohydrates 14g

Fennel Asparagus Salmon Bake

Preparation Time: 10 minutes

Cook Time: 30 minutes

Serves: 4 servings

Ingredients

Fennel fronds

1 tbsp extra virgin olive oil

1 tbsp lime juice, fresh

1 tsp Himalayan pink salt

1 tbsp kelp, dried

1 tbsp coconut aminos

1 tbsp coconut aminos

2 medium avocados, halves and slice

1/2 cup thinly sliced, fennel

2 cups asparagus

21 ounces wild salmon

Directions

1. In a big bowl, add lime juice, salt, honey, kelp, coconut aminos and salmon.

2. Stir and set aside to marinate for 20 minutes.

3. Heat up the oven to 350°F.

4. Add the asparagus into a steamer to steam and set aside to cool.

5. On a heat-proof oven tray, add on the sliced fennel and salmon.

6. Transfer the tray into the middle of the oven and bake until the salmon is well cooked for 10 minutes.

7. On a plate, add the sliced avocados, baked fennel and salmon.

8. Season with Himalayan salt and top with fennel fronds. Sprinkle olive oil over the salmon and fennel.

Nutritional Information/Serving

Calories 537.7 kcal, Fat 24.6g, Net Carbs 13.1g, Dietary Fiber 24.9g, Protein 50.9g

Chicken Fajitas (Keto Sheet Pan)

Preparation Time: 10 minutes

Cook Time: 25 minutes

Serves: 4 servings

Ingredients

Fresh lime juice

1 (thinly sliced) onion

1 (sliced) bell peppers

1 tablespoon taco seasoning

Olive oil

1.5 pounds boneless skinless chicken breasts (slice into strips)

Directions

1. Coat a big rimmed baking pan and heat up the oven to 400°F.

2. Add the chicken into a bowl and sprinkle taco seasoning over the chicken to coat.

3. Dribble olive oil over the seasoned chicken breast lightly.

4. In another bowl, add the sliced onion and bell pepper.

5. Sprinkle taco seasoning and olive oil over the vegetables in the bowl.

6. Transfer the vegetables and seasoned chicken onto the prepared baking pan.

7. Move the baking pan into the oven and bake for 20 minutes to 25 minutes until the vegetables are soft and the chicken is well cooked.

8. Take the pan from the oven and sprinkle the lime juice over the baked chicken and veggies.

9. Serve with cauliflower rice.

Nutritional Information/Serving

Calories 424 kcal, Protein 55.7g, Net Carbs 13.1g, Fiber 6g, Fat 13.9g

Keto Chicken Jar Salad

Preparation Time: 10 minutes

Cook Time: 0 minutes

Serves: 1 serving

Ingredients

1 cup (chopped) romaine lettuce

3 ounces (grilled & cubed) chicken breast

2 tablespoons (sliced) red onions

2/3 cup (chopped) cucumbers

2/3 cup (halved) grape tomatoes

1/4 teaspoon black pepper

1/2 teaspoon sea salt

2 teaspoons balsamic vinegar

2 tablespoons olive oil

Directions

1. Add black pepper, salt, balsamic vinegar and olive oil into a small airtight container and shake until the mixture combine to form a dressing.

2. In a big mason jar, add in the dressing to the base of the jar.

3. Add in the chopped lettuce, cubed chicken breast, sliced red onion, chopped cucumber and tomatoes.

Note: don't shake or stir until you are ready to serve.

4. Place lid over mason jar and place into the fridge for 3 days to 5 days.

5. Shake mason jar to mix the salad and serve in a bowl.

Nutritional Information/Serving

Calories 627 kcal, Dietary Fiber 3g, Net Carbs 10g, Protein 25g, Fat 52g

Keto Buffalo Turkey Meatballs

Preparation Time: 10 minutes

Cook Time: 15 minutes

Serves: 6 servings

Ingredients

1 tablespoon olive oil

1/2 cup buffalo sauce

1/2 cup (chopped) green onions

1/2 cup (crumbled) blue cheese

1/4 cup egg white

1 1/2 pounds turkey (ground)

Directions

1. Use silicone mat to line a baking pan and heat up the oven to 400°F.

2. In a bowl, add 3/4 cup of Buffalo sauce, green onions, blue cheese, egg white and turkey. Mix together.

3. Cut and roll out one-inch balls from the turkey mixture and arrange the balls on the prepared baking pan.

4. Transfer the baking pan into the oven and bake meatballs until it is just cooked, for 12 minutes to 15 minutes.

5. In another bowl, add olive oil and the remaining buffalo sauce. Whisk the mixture together.

6. Drain the baked meatballs fluid and place the drained meatballs on the parchment paper in the baking pan.

7. Dribble the buffalo sauce mixture (a small amount) over each meatball on the baking pan.

8. Transfer the baking pan into the oven and bake meatballs for 2 minutes to 3 minutes more.

Nutritional Information/Serving

Calories 332 kcal, Sugar 0.3g, Dietary Fiber 0.2g, Net Carbs 0.8g, Protein 34g, Fat 20g

Cheesy Bacon Jalapeno Poppers

Preparation Time: 10 minutes

Cook Time: 15 minutes

Serves: 12 servings

Ingredients

1/4 cup (pre-cooked) bacon bits

1 tablespoon (minced) fresh cilantro

2 cloves (minced) garlic

1/4 cup (chopped) green onions

3 ounces (softened) cream cheese

1/4 cup (shredded) cheddar cheese

6 medium (sliced lengthwise & seeded) jalapeno

Directions

1. Use foil to line a baking pan and heat up the oven to 400°F.

2. Add minced garlic, cilantro, green onions, cheddar cheese and cream cheese into a small bowl.

3. Stir the cream cheese mixture together.

4. Add the cream cheese mixture into the jalapeno halves and arrange on the prepared baking pan.

5. Add 1 tsp of bacon bits over each jalapeno popper.

6. Use the back of a spoon to lightly press down the bacon bits into the filling.

7. Transfer the baking pan into the oven.

8. Bake until the top of the bacon bits is crisped and the jalapenos are tender, for 15 minutes.

Nutritional Information/Serving

Calories 49 kcal, Sugar 0.3g, Dietary Fiber 0.3g, Net Carbs 0.7g, Total Carbs 1g, Protein 2g, Fat 4g

Cheesy Turkey Filled Mushrooms (Italian Keto)

Preparation Time: 10 minutes

Cook Time: 20 minutes

Serves: 5 servings

Ingredients

1/4 teaspoon black pepper

1/2 teaspoon sea salt

2 cloves (minced) garlic

1/4 cup (chopped) fresh basil

1 1/2 cup marinara sauce

1 cup (shredded) pepper Jack cheese

1 pound turkey (ground)

4 jumbo portobello mushrooms (caps only)

Directions

1. Use silicone mat to line a baking pan and heat up the oven to 375°F.

2. Add the mushrooms on the prepared baking pan, with the cavity facing up.

3. Transfer the baking pan into the oven and bake for 15 minutes to 20 minutes, until the mushrooms are tender.

4. At med-high heat, place a pan over heat and add in the ground turkey.

5. Stir-cook the turkey, for 7 minutes to 10 minutes until the turkey is golden.

6. At med-heat, add the minced garlic into the pan with the turkey and cook until aromatic for a minute.

7. Add in black pepper, salt, basil and marinara sauce into the pan. Taste and adjust black pepper and salt as desired.

8. Cook marinara sauce mixture, until it is well heated, for 2 minutes to 3 minutes.

9. Drain off any liquid from the mushroom caps and fill it with the turkey mixture.

10. Add Jack cheese over the turkey mixture to top.

11. Place the filled mushroom caps onto the baking pan and place the pan on the rack.

12. Broil for 3 minutes until the cheese is lightly golden and melted.

Nutritional Information/Serving

Calories 336 kcal, Sugar 4g, Dietary Fiber 2g, Net Carbs 6g, Protein 33g, Fat 19g

Mexican Coconut Flour Wraps

Preparation Time: 5 minutes

Cook Time: 10 minutes

Serves: 12 servings

Ingredients

1/2 teaspoon paprika

1/2 teaspoon cumin

3/4 teaspoon sea salt

1 1/4 cups coconut milk

6 large eggs

1/2 cup coconut flour

Directions

1. Add paprika, cumin, salt, coconut milk, eggs and coconut flour into a big bowl.

2. Whisk until a fine texture is formed. Set aside the batter for 2 minutes.

Note: The batter should be easy to pour.

3. At med-heat, place an 8" small pan over heat and grease the pan with oil lightly.

4. Add batter (1/4 cup) into the pan and tilt immediately to distribute evenly.

5. Place lid over pan and cook until the center starts to form bubbles and the ends are brown.

6. Turn the batter and cook for a minute or 2 minutes, until the other side is golden.

7. Repeat the above process with the remaining batter.

Nutritional Information/Serving

Calories 55 kcal, Dietary Fiber 3g, Net Carbs 1g, Protein 5g, Fat 3g

Russian Radish Salad with Creamy Herb Dressing

Preparation Time: 10 minutes

Cook Time: 0 minutes

Serves: 4 servings

Ingredients (Salad)

2 cups (thinly sliced) radish

2 cups (cut in half and cut off the edges) sugar snap peas

Dressing

Black pepper

Garlic salt

1 tablespoon (chopped) fresh dill

1 teaspoon olive oil

1 teaspoon white vinegar

1/4 cup sour cream

Directions

1. In a medium bowl, add radish and sugar snap peas. Mix together.

2. In a small bowl, add dill, olive oil, white vinegar and sour cream.

3. Add in black pepper and salt to season the sour cream mixture as desired.

4. Whisk the sour cream together.

5. Sprinkle the dressing over the radish mixture and toss until it is combined.

6. Add more fresh dill to garnish the salad. Serve.

Nutritional Information/Serving

Calories 74 kcal, Dietary Fiber 2g, Net Carbs 5g, Protein 2g, Fat 4g

Cheese Mushrooms Beef Squash Boats

Preparation Time: 10 minutes

Cook Time: 30 minutes

Serves: 6 servings

Ingredients

3/4 cup (shredded and divided in two) swiss cheese

2 tablespoons sour cream

1/2 teaspoon black pepper

3/4 teaspoon sea salt

1 pound beef, ground

4 cloves (minced) garlic

4 ounces (chopped) shiitake mushrooms

1/2 large (chopped) white onion

1 teaspoon olive oil

3 large zucchinis (slice length-wise)

Directions

1. Use foil to line a baking pan and heat up the oven to 400°F.

2. Make a hollow in each zucchini half with a small spoon.

3. On the prepared baking pan, add the zucchini, cut side up. Lightly season zucchini with salt.

4. Transfer the baking pan into the oven and bake until the zucchini is almost tender, for 15 minutes to 20 minutes.

5. At med-heat, place a pan over heat and add olive oil.

6. Add in the chopped onion to the pan and stir-cook until it is lightly brown and translucent, for 7 minutes to 10 minutes.

7. Add in minced garlic and mushrooms, Stir-cook until the mushroom reduces in size and is lightly golden, for 5 minutes to 7 minutes.

8. Increase heat to med-high heat, and add beef into the pan.

9. Sprinkle black pepper and salt over the ground beef.

10. Cook until the chopped onion is caramelized, and the ground beef is golden, for 7 minutes to 8 minutes.

11. Use a spoon to break the ground beef into pieces.

12. Take the pan off heat, add in half of the swiss cheese and sour cream. Stir together.

13. Scoop the ground beef mixture into each zucchini halves.

14. Bake zucchini halves until the filling releases bubbles and the zucchini is well cooked for 10 minutes.

15. Set oven to broil, and add the other half of the swiss cheese over the zucchini boats.

16. Broil until the swiss cheese is golden and melts for 3 minutes.

Nutritional Information/Serving

Calories 245 kcal, Dietary Fiber 0.4g, Net carbs 3.6g, Protein 18g, Fat 17g

Avocado Bacon Broccoli Salad

Preparation Time: 10 minutes

Cook Time: 0 minutes

Serves: 8 servings

Ingredients

Black pepper (a pinch)

1/4 teaspoon garlic salt

1 teaspoon white vinegar

1 tablespoon olive oil

1/2 cup mayo

1 large (cubed) avocado

1/2 cup (shredded) cheddar cheese

1/4 cup (cooked) bacon bits

1/4 large (finely chopped) red onion

1 bunch (chopped into small florets) broccoli

Directions

1. In a big bowl, add the shredded cheddar cheese, cooked bacon bits, chopped red onion and chopped broccoli. Mix together.

2. Add black pepper, garlic salt, white vinegar, olive oil and mayo into a small bowl.

3. Whisk the mayo mixture together until a fine texture is reached.

4. Transfer the dressing mixture into the cheddar cheese/broccoli bowl and mix together until it is combined.

5. Fold in the cubed avocado and serve.

Nutritional Information/Serving

Calories 224 kcal, Dietary Fiber 3g, Net Carbs 4g, Protein 6g, Fat 20g

Garlic Cheese Mushrooms

Preparation Time: 10 minutes

Cook Time: 20 minutes

Serves: 6 servings

Ingredients

Black pepper

Sea salt

1 tablespoon (minced) fresh parsley

4 cloves (minced) garlic

1/2 cup (crumbled) feta cheese

8 ounces (chopped) spinach

1 tablespoon olive oil

24 baby portobello mushrooms (removed stems)

Directions

1. Use parchment paper to line a baking pan and heat up the oven to 400°F.

2. Add few tablespoons of water and the chopped spinach into a bowl.

3. Use plastic wrap to cover the spinach bowl and place into a microwave to cook until the spinach wilts, for 2 minutes.

4. Transfer the spinach into a colander over the sink to drain the liquid, and let stand until completely cool.

5. On the prepared baking pan, arrange mushrooms, stem side up, in a layer and dribble olive oil over the mushroom's cavity.

6. Sprinkle black pepper and salt over the mushroom's cavity to season.

7. Squeeze the drained spinach tightly until the remaining liquid is drained.

Note: The drained spinach will form a tight ball and reduce in size.

8. Add minced fresh parsley, minced garlic, crumbled feta cheese and the drained spinach into a medium bowl. Mix together.

9. Sprinkle black pepper and salt over the spinach mixture to taste as needed.

10. Share the spinach mixture into the 24 mushrooms cavities on the baking pan.

11. Place the baking pan into the oven and bake until mushrooms are brown and tender, for 15 minutes to 20 minutes.

Nutritional Information/Serving

Calories 82 kcal, Dietary Fiber 1g, Net Carbs 4g, Protein 4g, Fat 5g

Herbed Chicken Salad with Mayo

Preparation Time: 10 minutes

Cook Time: 0 minutes

Serves: 8 servings

Ingredients

Black pepper

Sea salt

1/2 cup (chopped) green onions

3 cups (cooked) shredded chicken

2 cloves (minced) garlic

2 tablespoons (chopped) fresh parsley

2 tablespoons (chopped) fresh dill

2 tablespoons mustard

1/4 cup mayo

Directions

1. In a bowl, add minced garlic, parsley, dill, mustard and mayo.

2. Stir together until a fine texture is formed.

3. Add in green onions and shredded chicken into the mayo bowl and stir together.

4. Sprinkle black pepper and salt over the chicken mixture.

5. Transfer the bowl with the salad into the refrigerator for 2 hours and serve.

Nutritional Information/Serving

Calories 123 kcal, Dietary Fiber 0.4g, Net Carbs 2.6g, Protein 11g, Fat 8g

Brussel Sprouts Bacon Au Gratin

Preparation Time: 10 minutes

Cook Time: 45 minutes

Serves: 10 servings

Ingredients

1/4 cup bacon bits

1 1/2 cup (shredded) cheddar cheese

2 tablespoons butter

1/2 cup heavy cream

1/2 cup unsweetened almond milk

1/2 teaspoon black pepper (divided into two)

1 teaspoon sea salt (scant)

1 tablespoon olive oil

2 pounds (halved) brussels sprouts

Directions

1. Use silicone mats to line two baking pans of 13 by 9" and heat up the oven to 400°F.

2. In a bowl, add olive oil and brussels sprouts.

3. Toss, and sprinkle black pepper and 1/2 teaspoon of salt over the coated brussels sprouts. Toss again to coat.

4. Lay the coated brussels sprouts on the prepared baking pans in a layer.

5. Transfer the baking pans into the oven and bake on both sides until the ends are crisped and golden, for 35 minutes to 45 minutes. Rotate halfway through baking.

6. In a microwaveable bowl, add in butter and place the butter bowl into the microwave. Cook until the butter melts.

7. Add in heavy cream and unsweetened almond milk into the butter bowl.

8. Return the butter bowl into the microwave and cook until the mixture is hot.

9. Add in a cup of cheddar cheese into the almond milk bowl and stir until the cheese melts.

10. Sprinkle black pepper and 1/2 teaspoon of salt over the cheddar cheese mixture.

11. Line a small baking sheet of 9 by 9" and transfer the baked brussels sprouts onto the baking sheet.

12. Pour the cheese mixture over the baked brussels sprouts on the baking sheet.

13. Sprinkle 1/2 cup of cheddar cheese and bacon bits over the sauce on the brussels sprouts.

14. Transfer the baking sheet into the oven and bake until the cheese releases bubbles, for 10 minutes to 15 minutes.

Nutritional Information/Serving

Calories 196 kcal, Dietary Fiber 3g, Net Carbs 5g, Protein 8g, Fat 15g

Keto-Japanese Kani Salad

Preparation Time: 10 minutes

Cook Time: 0 minutes

Serves: 4 servings

Ingredients (Dressing)

1 teaspoon sriracha

1 teaspoon sesame oil (toasted)

1 teaspoon lemon juice

1/4 cup mayo

Salad

1/2 cup (slice into matchstick pieces) carrots

1/2 cup (slice into matchstick pieces) cucumber

12 ounces (rinsed in warm water until tender) Kelp noodles

8 ounces lump crab meat

Directions

1. In a bowl, add sriracha, sesame oil, lemon juice and mayo.

2. Whisk the lemon juice mixture together.

3. Add the crab meat, carrots, cucumber and kelp noodles into a large bowl.

4. Stir the dressing into the crab meat mixture.

5. Serve with desired keto garnishes

Nutritional Information/Serving

Calories 169 kcal, Dietary Fiber 1g, Net Carbs 3g, Protein 12g, Fat 12g

Mozzarella Spinach Filled Chicken

Preparation Time: 10 minutes

Cook Time: 20 minutes

Serves: 4 servings

Ingredients

Black pepper

Sea salt

1 medium (sliced into 8 thinly slices) roma tomato

2 ounces cream cheese

4 ounces (shredded and divided) mozzarella cheese

2 cloves (minced) garlic

6 ounces (chopped) spinach

4 large chicken breasts

Direction

1. Use foil to line a baking pan and heat up the oven to 450°F.

2. Add salt and water into a big bowl.

3. Add chicken breast into the salt water and fully submerge the chicken.

4. Allow the chicken to brine, for 10 minutes.

5. Add the chopped spinach into a microwaveable bowl and cook until it is wilted, for 2 minutes to 3 minutes.

6. Set aside the cooked spinach to cool and drain the moisture completely.

7. Transfer the drained spinach into a bowl.

8. Divide the mozzarella cheese into half, add into the spinach bowl and top with minced garlic.

9. Add cream cheese into a bowl and microwave until it melts.

10. Stir in the melted cream cheese into the spinach bowl and mix.

11. Pat dry the chicken with paper towel, and transfer it onto the lined baking pan.

12. Create a pocket in the chicken breast by horizontally cutting a slit on each side of the chicken.

13. Add the spinach mixture into the chicken pocket by stuffing the mixture into it.

14. Season the chicken with black pepper and salt.

15. Add the remaining mozzarella cheese and two Roma tomato slices to top each chicken pieces.

16. Transfer the pan into the oven and bake until the chicken is well cooked, for 16 minutes to 20 minutes.

Note: Tent the chicken with foil if the cheese becomes golden too early.

Nutritional Information/Serving

Calories 336 kcal, Dietary Fiber 0g, Net Carbs 3g, Protein 47g, Fat 13g

Tasty Italian Meatballs

Preparation Time: 15 minutes

Cook Time: 15 minutes

Serves: 6 servings

Ingredients

3/4 cup marinara sauce

1 pound beef (ground)

2 tablespoons (chopped) fresh parsley

3 cloves (minced) garlic

1 large egg

3 tablespoons (grated) onion

1/4 cup heavy cream

1/2 teaspoon black pepper

3/4 teaspoon sea salt

1 tablespoon Italian seasoning

1/4 cup almond flour

1/4 cup parmesan cheese (grated)

Directions

1. Use Foil to line a baking pan and grease the foil. Heat up the oven to 425°F.

2. Add black pepper, salt, Italian seasoning, almond flour and parmesan cheese into a big bowl.

3. Stir the almond flour mixture together.

4. In a bowl, add parsley, garlic, egg, onion and heavy cream.

5. Whisk together and add into the almond flour bowl.

6. Set the mixture aside for some minutes.

7. Add the ground beef into the almond flour bowl, and mix with hands to lightly combine the mixture.

8. Form 1-inch balls from the mixture and arrange on the lined baking pan.

9. Transfer the baking pan into the prepared oven and bake until the meatballs are just baked, for 10 minutes to 12 minutes.

10. Transfer the baking pan under a broiler.

11. Broil for couple of minutes until the meatballs are golden.

12. Add marinara sauce over each meatball and return the baking pan into the oven.

13. Bake meatballs until the meatballs are well cooked, and marinara sauce is hot, for 3 minutes to 5 minutes.

14. Serve and add more parsley to garnish.

Nutritional Information/Serving

Calories 324 kcal, Dietary Fiber 1g, Net Carbs 4g, Protein 25g, Fat 22g

DINNER

Chinese Hot & Sour Soup

Preparation Time: 5 minutes

Cook Time: 15 minutes

Serves: 6 servings

Ingredients

White pepper

Kosher salt

1 tsp sesame oil (toasted)

4 (thinly sliced) green onions (divided into two)

8 oz (cut into 1/2" cubes) firm tofu

2 large (whisked) eggs

1/4 cup cornstarch

1 tsp chili garlic sauce

2 tsps ginger (ground)

1/4 cup soy sauce (reduced-sodium)

1/4 cup rice vinegar,

8 oz (discard the stem & thinly sliced) baby Bella mushrooms

8 cups vegetable stock

Directions

1. In a big stock pot, add in garlic sauce, ginger, soy sauce, rice wine vinegar, mushrooms and 7 3/4 cups of vegetables stock.

2. Stir the vegetable stock mixture until combined.

3. At med-high heat, place the stock pot over heat and cook until soup reaches a simmer.

4. In a small bowl, add in cornstarch and the remaining vegetable stock. Whisk together until a fine texture is reached.

5. Add the vegetable mixture into the soup and Stir until soup thicken for a minute.

6. In a circular motion, stir the soup and cook.

7. To form egg ribbons, dribble the whisked eggs into the soup while you stir the soup.

8. Add in the sesame oil, green onion (half) and tofu into the soup. Stir together.

9. Sprinkle white pepper and salt into the soup.

10. Add the remaining green onions to garnish the soup.

Nutritional Information/Serving

Calories 96 kcal, Protein 8.1g, Dietary Fiber 1.9g, Net Carbs 6.8g, Fat 4.3g

Scrumptious Keto Steak Fajitas

Preparation Time: 5 minutes

Cook Time: 15 minutes

Serves: 5 servings

Ingredients

1 (sliced) yellow pepper

1 (sliced) red pepper

750g steak

1 lemon juice (include zest)

1 lime juice (include zest)

60 ml olive oil

Pepper

Salt

1 tablespoon cumin powder (ground)

0.5 teaspoon chilli powder

1 onion (thinly sliced)

2 cloves (crushed) garlic

Directions

1. In a bowl, add yellow pepper, red pepper, steak, lemon juice, pepper, salt, cumin powder, chilli powder, onion and garlic.

2. Mix until the steak mixture combines.

3. Transfer the steak mixture onto a baking tray.

4. Heat up the oven to 350°F.

5. Place the baking tray with the steak mixture into the oven and bake for 15 minutes.

6. Stir the steak mixture half way while baking.

Note: The fajitas will be thoroughly combined and well cooked.

7. Serve and drizzle olive oil and lime juice over the fajitas.

Nutritional Information/Serving

Calories 440 kcal, Protein 31g, Dietary Fiber 1g, Carbohydrates 5g, Fat 33g

Slow Cooker Beef Soup Recipe

Preparation Time: 15 minutes

Cook Time: 4 hours

Serves: 14 servings

Ingredients

1/2 teaspoon garlic powder

1 tablespoon Italian seasoning

6 cups vegetable broth

1 (15 ounces) can diced tomatoes (include the liquid)

1 pound coleslaw mix (shredded)

1/4 teaspoon black pepper

1 teaspoon sea salt

1 pound beef, ground

1 large (chopped) onion

1 tablespoon coconut oil

Directions

1. At med-heat, place a big skillet over heat and add coconut oil.

2. Add onions into the skillet and stir-cook until the onions are just golden for 10 minutes to 15 minutes.

3. Add in the beef and sprinkle black pepper and salt over the ground beef.

4. Saute the ground beef until it is golden for 7 minutes to 10 minutes on med-high heat, and use a spatula to break the beef into smaller portions.

5. In a slow cooker, add garlic powder, Italian seasoning, vegetable broth, tomatoes and shredded coleslaw mix.

6. Transfer the cooked beef mixture into the slow cooker and stir the mixture until it combines.

7. Taste mixture and sprinkle additional black pepper and salt as needed.

8. Cook on high for 2 hours to 3 hours or on low for 5 hours to 6 hours.

Nutritional Information/Serving

Calories 111 kcal, Dietary Fiber 1g, Net Carbs 4g, Protein 9g, Fat 6g

Slow Cooker Chicken Buffalo Soup

Preparation Time: 10 minutes

Cook Time: 3 hours

Serves: 6 servings

Ingredients

1/2 cup heavy cream

6 ounces (at room temperature & cubed) cream cheese

3 tablespoons buffalo sauce

4 cup chicken broth

1 pound (cooked & shredded) chicken

4 cloves (minced) garlic

1/2 cup (diced) celery

1/2 large (diced) onion

1 tablespoon olive oil

Directions

1. At med-heat, place a skillet over heat and add a tbsp of olive oil.

2. Add in diced celery and onion into the heated oil in the skillet.

3. Stir-cook until the onions are just golden and translucent for 5 minutes to 10 minutes.

4. Add in the minced garlic and saute until aromatic for 1 minute.

5. In a slow cooker, add buffalo sauce, chicken broth and the cooked chicken.

6. Transfer the onion mixture into the slow cooker and stir with the chicken mixture.

7. Cook the chicken mixture in the slow cooker for 3 hours to 4 hours on low.

8. Scoop 1 cup of the chicken juice and pour it into an electric blender.

9. Add in cream cheese into the blender and puree the mixture until a fine texture is reached.

10. Stir in the cream cheese mixture into the slow cooker and add in heavy cream.

11. Stir the soup until a fine texture is formed.

Nutritional Information/Serving

Calories 270 kcal, Dietary Fiber 0.4g, Net Carbs 3.6g, Protein 27g, Fat 16g

Mozzarella Pizza Casserole
Preparation Time: 10 minutes

Cook Time: 40 minutes

Serves: 6 servings

Ingredients

2 ounces pepperoni slices

2 cup (shredded) mozzarella cheese

1 1/2 cup marinara sauce

Black pepper

Sea salt

2 tablespoons olive oil

1 large (cut into small florets) cauliflower head

Directions

1. Heat up the oven to 425°F.

2. Add black pepper, salt, olive oil and the cauliflower florets into a glass casserole dish of 13 by 9".

3. Toss to coat the cauliflower florets and arrange the cauliflower in a layer.

4. Transfer the dish into the oven and bake until it is a lightly brown for 25 minutes.

5. Sprinkle the marinara sauce over the baked cauliflower and add the mozzarella cheese.

6. Add pepperoni slices over the mozzarella cheese and return the dish into the oven.

7. Bake until the cheese is brown and melt completely for 10 minutes.

Nutritional Information/Serving

Calories 238 kcal, Dietary Fiber 3g, Net Carbs 7g, Protein 14g, Fat 16g

Italian Cheesy Eggplant Lasagna

Preparation Time: 20 minutes

Cook Time: 40 minutes

Serves: 8 servings

Ingredients

Black pepper

Sea salt

2 tablespoons olive oil

1 1/4 pound eggplant, medium (sliced lengthways into 8 slices, about 1/2"
to 1/4" thin)

1 tablespoon Italian seasoning

1 1/2 cup marinara sauce

1/2 teaspoon black pepper

1 teaspoon sea salt

1 1/2 pounds beef (ground)

2 cloves (minced) garlic

1 teaspoon olive oil

Filling

1 large egg

1/2 cup parmesan cheese, grated

8 ounces ricotta cheese

Topping

2 cup mozzarella cheese

Directions

1. At med-heat, place a big skillet over heat and add oil.

2. Add in minced garlic into the skillet and saute until aromatic, for 30 seconds.

3. Add in the beef, sprinkle black pepper and salt over the beef to season.

4. Saute for 10 minutes, until the beef is golden. Use a spatula to break the beef apart.

5. Add in the Italian seasoning and marinara sauce into the skillet and stir together.

6. Simmer the sauce for 10 minutes.

7. Line a big baking pan and grease it. Heat up the oven to 400°F.

8. On the prepared pan, lay the eggplant slices in a layer. Use olive oil to brush both sides of the slices.

9. Sprinkle black pepper and salt over the eggplant slices to season.

10. Transfer the baking pan into the oven and bake until the eggplant becomes tender, for 15 minutes.

11. Take the baking pan out of the oven and leave the oven on.

12. Add egg, parmesan cheese, ricotta cheese into a small bowl and stir together.

13. Line the base of a stoneware casserole dish of 13 by 9", and arrange the baked eggplant slices into the dish, in a layer.

14. Add the sauteed ground beef mixture over the eggplant slices in the dish.

15. Add in the ricotta cheese mixture over the beef mixture in the dish and spread.

16. Sprinkle the mozzarella cheese over the ricotta cheese.

17. Repeat the arrangement in the dish with the remaining ingredients and top with the mozzarella cheese.

18. Transfer the dish into the oven and bake until the mozzarella cheese is browned and melted, for 15 minutes.

Nutritional Information/Serving

Calories 426 kcal, Dietary Fiber 3g, Net Carbs 6g, Protein 30g, Fat 30g

Low Carb Fathead Pizza Crust

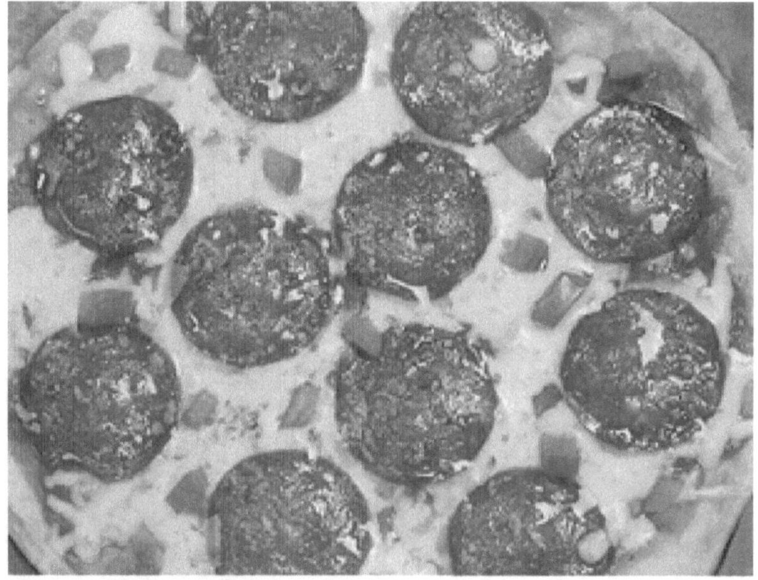

Preparation Time: 10 minutes

Cook Time: 10 minutes

Serves: 8 servings

Ingredients

1/3 cup coconut flour

2 large (beaten) egg

2 tablespoons (cut into cubes) cream cheese

1 1/2 cup (shredded) mozzarella cheese

Directions

1. Use parchment paper to line a pizza pan and heat up the oven to 425°F.

2. In a big bowl, add the cream cheese and mozzarella cheese.

3. Transfer the cheese bowl into the microwave and cook for 45 seconds.

4. Stir the cheeses and cook again for another 45 seconds until it is combined.

5. In a bowl, add the coconut flour and eggs.

6. Stir in the coconut flour mixture into the cheese bowl.

7. Use hands to knead the dough on a work surface until a doughy texture is formed.

Note: Microwave the dough for 10 seconds to 15 seconds until tender, if it is hard while kneading.

8. Transfer the dough onto the prepared pizza pan and spread evenly to form 1/4 thickness.

9. Poke several holes throughout the crust with a toothpick.

Note: The holes will prevent bubble formation in the crust while baking.

10. Transfer the pizza pan into the oven and bake crust for 6 minutes.

11. Remove the pan from the oven and poke anywhere bubble is found on the crust.

13. Return the pan into the oven and bake until the pizza crust is golden brown, for 3 minutes to 7 minutes.

Calories 117 kcal, Dietary Fiber 2g, Net Carbs 2g, Protein 7g, Fat 8g

Keto Cream of Mushroom Soup

Preparation Time: 5 minutes

Cook Time: 30 minutes

Serves: 5 servings

Ingredients

1/4 teaspoon black pepper

3/4 teaspoon sea salt

1 cup coconut milk

1 cup coconut cream

2 cups chicken broth

6 cloves (minced) garlic

20 ounces (sliced) mushrooms

1/2 large (diced) onion

1 tablespoon avocado oil

Directions

1. At med-heat, place a big pot over heat and add in olive oil, sliced mushroom and the diced onions.

2. Stir-cook until the onions are lightly golden, for 10 minutes to 15 minutes.

3. Add in the minced garlic, and cook for 1 minute.

4. Add in black pepper, salt, coconut milk, coconut cream and chicken broth into the pot with the mushroom mixture.

5. Boil the mushroom mixture, and then simmer while you stir occasionally for 15 minutes.

6. Puree the mushroom mixture with an immersion blender until a fine texture is formed.

Nutritional Information/Serving

Calories 229 kcal, Dietary Fiber 2g, Net Carbs 6g, Protein 5g, Fat 21g

Tasty Shredded Chicken Soup with Spaghetti Squash

Preparation Time: 10 minutes

Cook Time: 1 hour

Serves: 14 servings

Ingredients

1 medium spaghetti squash

Black pepper

Sea salt

1 medium (whole) bay leaf

1 tablespoon Italian seasoning

10 cups chicken broth

1 cup (diced) onion

1 cup (diced) celery

1 cup (diced) carrots

2 cups (cooked) chicken, shredded

Directions

1. Add black pepper, salt, bay leaf, Italian seasoning, chicken broth, onion, celery, carrots and shredded chicken into a big pot.

2. Boil the chicken broth mixture, reduce heat and simmer for an hour.

3. Use a sharp knife to poke several holes in spaghetti squash. Heat up the oven to 375°F.

4. Transfer the spaghetti squash onto a baking pan and bake until a fork can pierce the skin easily, for 40 minutes to 60 minutes.

Note: If the spaghetti squash is over baked it will become mushy. Avoid over baking.

5. Set the spaghetti squash aside after baking, to cool. Cut into two equal part and scoop out the strands with a fork.

6. Take out the bay leaf from the soup and add in half of the spaghetti squash strands.

Nutritional Information/Serving

Calories 44 kcal, Dietary Fiber 1g, Net Carbs 3g, Protein 5g, Fat 1g

Tasty Beef Chili

Preparation Time: 15 minutes

Cook Time: 8 hours

Serves: 10 servings

Ingredients

1 teaspoon black pepper

2 teaspoons sea salt

1 tablespoon oregano (dried)

2 tablespoons cumin

1/4 cup chili powder

2 tablespoons Worcestershire sauce

1 (4-ounces) can (include the liquid) green chiles

1 (6-ounces) can tomato paste

2 (15-ounces) can (include the liquid) diced tomatoes

8 cloves (minced) garlic

1/2 large (chopped) onion

2 1/2 pounds beef (ground)

Directions

1. At med-high heat, place a skillet over heat and add in the onion.

2. Saute until the onion becomes translucent, for 5 minutes to 7 minutes.

3. Add in the minced garlic to the skillet and saute until aromatic for 1 minute.

4. Add in the beef and saute until it is golden, for 8 minutes to 10 minutes.

5. Use a spatula to break the ground beef apart.

6. In a slow cooker, add in black pepper, salt, oregano, cumin, chili powder, Worcestershire sauce, green chiles, tomato paste and diced tomatoes.

7. Add the beef mixture to the slow cooker with the diced tomatoes mixture, and stir until it combines.

8. Cook on high for 3 hours to 4 hours or on low for 6 hours to 8 hours.

Nutritional Information/Serving

Calories 306 kcal, Dietary Fiber 3g, Net Carbs 10g, Protein 23g, Fat 18g

Slow Cooker Chuck Roast Recipe

Preparation Time: 10 minutes

Cook Time: 4 hours

Serves: 9 servings

Ingredients

2 whole bay leaf

1/2 teaspoon cloves (ground)

1 teaspoon black pepper

2 teaspoons sea salt

2 teaspoons cumin

1 tablespoon (dried) oregano

2 tablespoons lime juice

2 tablespoons apple cider vinegar

5 cloves (minced) garlic

2 medium (include about 4 teaspoons of the sauce) chipotle chiles in adobo

1/2 cup chicken broth

3 pounds (trimmed & cut into 2" chunks) chuck roast

Directions

1. In a blender, add ground cloves, black pepper, salt, cumin, oregano, lime juice, vinegar, minced garlic, chipotle chiles in adobo and the chicken broth.

2. Blend until a fine texture is reached.

3. In a slow cooker, add in the chuck roast and the pureed lime juice mixture.

4. Add in the bay leaf and cook until the chuck roast is soft and begins to fall apart, on low for 8 hours to 10 hours, or on high for 4 hours to 6 hours.

5. Take out the bay leaves, and use 2 forks to shred the chuck roast.

6. Stir the shredded chuck roast into the cooking juices.

7. Cover the slow cooker and set aside until flavor is infused, for 5 minutes to 10 minutes.

8. Serve with a slotted spoon.

Nutritional Information/Serving

Calories 242 kcal, Dietary Fiber 1g, Net Carbs 1g, Protein 32g, Fat 11g

Beefy Cauliflower Casserole

Preparation Time: 10 minutes

Cook Time: 30 minutes

Serves: 8 servings

Ingredients

Black pepper

Sea salt

1 cup (shredded) mozzarella cheese

1/2 cup (chopped and divided) fresh basil

14.5 ounces can diced tomatoes

1 cup marinara sauce

2 cloves (minced) garlic

1/2 large (chopped) Onion

1 pound beef (ground)

1 tablespoon olive oil

1 head (cut into florets) cauliflower

Directions

1. Grease a round casserole dish of 9" lightly and heat up the oven to 400°F.

2. In a bowl, add cauliflower and olive oil. Toss to coat.

3. Lightly season the coated cauliflower with black pepper and salt.

4. Transfer the cauliflower into the prepared casserole dish.

5. Place the dish into the oven and bake until it is soft and crispy, for 15 minutes to 20 minutes. Stir halfway through the baking.

6. At med-low heat, place a pan over heat and add the chopped onion.

7. Saute the onion until it is lightly golden and translucent for 8 minutes to 10 minutes.

8. Add beef into the pan and saute on med-high heat until the beef is golden, for 8 minutes to 10 minutes.

9. Use a spatula to break the beef apart while cooking.

10. Add 1/4 cup of basil, diced tomatoes, marinara sauce and the minced garlic into the pan.

11. Sprinkle black pepper and salt over the mixture in the pan and cook until it is well heated, for 2 minutes.

12. Stir in the sauce over the baked cauliflower.

13. Sprinkle mozzarella cheese over the sauce and transfer into the oven.

14. Bake until the mozzarella cheese releases bubbles, for 8 minutes to 10 minutes.

15. Add the remaining 1/4 cup of basil to top.

Nutritional Information/Serving

Calories 275 kcal, Dietary Fiber 3g, Net Carbs 8g, Protein 21g, Fat 17g

Chicken Coconut Curry

Preparation Time: 10 minutes

Cook Time: 25 minutes

Serves: 4 servings

Ingredients

Olive oil

1/3 cup red onion (diced)

4 tsps red curry paste

1 1/4 cups coconut milk

1 1/2 pounds (24 ounces) lean chicken thighs (raw & trim fat)

Garnish

Cilantro (fresh)

Pepper

Sea salt

Directions

1. Preheat the oven to 400°F.

2. Add the chicken thighs into a bowl and sprinkle red curry paste (two tsps) over the chicken.

3. Rub the curry with the chicken thighs and place the chicken bowl into the refrigerator for 20 minutes.

4. On med-heat, place a pan over heat, spray olive oil into the pan and heat up.

5. Add in the remaining red curry paste and onions into the heated oil.

6. Saute onions until it is lightly golden, for 3 minutes to 5 minutes.

7. Remove the chicken bowl from the refrigerator and transfer the chicken thighs into the pan.

8. Sear the chicken, for 2 minutes to 3 minutes.

9. Turn the chicken and add in 1 1/4 cups of coconut milk.

10. On low-heat, simmer the chicken mixture and transfer the pan with the chicken into the preheated oven.

11. Bake the chicken, for 12 minutes to 15 minutes and broil chicken for 2 minutes.

12. Serve coconut chicken curry and garnish with salt, pepper and fresh cilantro.

Nutritional Information/Serving

Calories 370 kcal, Dietary Fiber 0g, Carbohydrates 2g, Fat 25g, Protein 33g

Kale Turkey Soup

Preparation Time: 15 minutes

Cook Time: 15 minutes

Serves: 4 servings

Ingredients (meatballs)

2 tablespoons coconut oil

Fresh black pepper (ground)

3/4 teaspoon salt

2 tablespoons cilantro (fresh)

1/4 teaspoon garlic powder

2–4 tablespoons cassava flour

1 egg, beaten

1 lb. turkey (ground)

Soup

1 bunch (stem removed & chopped) kale

6 cups vegetables broth

2 bay leaves

2 cloves (minced) garlic

4 large (chopped) carrots

1 (diced) onion,

2 tablespoons ghee

Garnish

Red pepper flakes

Fresh dill (chopped)

Directions

1. Add the ground turkey, fresh cilantro, salt, garlic powder, cassava flour and beaten egg into a big bowl.

2. Stir the turkey mixture until it is combined.

3. Divide the turkey mixture and roll into 1 1/2" small balls.

Note: The total number of the small meatballs should be 24.

4. On med-high heat, place a big pan and add in coconut oil.

5. Add in meatballs into the heated coconut oil and cook until the sides are golden, for 3 minutes to 4 minutes.

Note: Cook meatballs in batches and let stand.

6. Place a big soup pot over heat. Add in ghee, minced garlic, carrots and diced onion into the pot.

7. Cook carrot mixture for 5 minutes, until the onion becomes translucent.

8. Add in the cooked meatballs, vegetables broth and bay leaves into the pot.

9. Boil the meatball mixture and reduce the heat. For 5 minutes, simmer soup.

10. Add in the chopped kale to the pot.

11. Cook the soup for 5 minutes to 7 minutes, until the soup is well cooked.

12. Serve and top with red pepper flakes and chopped dill.

Nutritional Information/Serving

Calories 441 kcal, Protein 27.0g, Dietary Fiber 5.7g, Carbohydrates 26.7g, Fat 24.0g

Coodles with Roasted Fennel Salmon

Preparation Time: 5 minutes

Cook Time: 15 minutes

Serves: 2 servings

Ingredients

2 tbsps extra virgin olive oil

Fresh thyme leaves

3 tbsps butter

1/2 cup green olives, pitted

1 big cucumber, (spiralize into noodles)

1 coarsely sliced, fennel bulb

2 (5-oz) wild salmon fillets with skin

Directions

1. Use a parchment paper to line a baking sheet and add fennel. Heat up the oven to 350°F.

2. Add the salmon fillets on top the fennel and use butter to make dots on the salmon fillet.

3. On the salmon filets, add thyme leaves.

4. Transfer the baking sheet into the oven and bake for 15 minutes.

5. Lightly squeeze the spiralized cucumber to remove excess water.

6. In a bowl, transfer the cucumber and sprinkle olive oil over it.

7. Take the baking sheet from the oven and serve the baked salmon fillets with the coodles.

8. Season with salt and add pitted green olives.

Nutritional Information/Serving

Calories 502.4 kcal, Fat 31.6g, Net Carbs 8.6g, Dietary Fiber 5.32g, Protein 38.9g

Ketogenic Chicken Salsa Soup

Preparation Time: 5 minutes

Cook Time: 30 minutes

Serves: 7 servings

Ingredients

4 tsps taco seasoning mix

1 1/2 cups mild salsa

8 oz cream cheese

3 cups low sodium chicken broth

1 lb. chicken breasts, boneless skinless

Topping

2 tbsps parsley (chopped)

1 (thinly diced) avocado

1/2 cup cheddar cheese (shredded)

Directions

1. In a bowl, divide the cream cheese into eight cubes and let stand.

2. In a pressure pot, add the seasoning mix, mild salsa and the chicken broth.

3. Mix until it combined and add in the boneless skinless chicken breasts into the liquid in the pressure pot.

4. Cover the pressure pot, saute chicken for 25 minutes on high.

5. Release pressure naturally for some minutes and then quick release. Move the cooked chicken into a bowl. Set aside to cool.

6. Add a cup of the hot liquid and cream cheese into a measuring glass.

7. Whisk the cream cheese mixture until a fine texture is reached for few minutes.

8. In a pot, add in the smooth cream cheese mixture. Mix and cook on med-heat.

9. Shred the cooked chicken in a bowl with two forks and transfer into the pot with the cream cheese mixture.

10. For few minutes, stir-cook to boil and serve.

11. Add the chopped parsley, shredded cheddar cheese and diced avocado
to the chicken soup.

Nutritional Information/Serving

Calories 311 kcal, Protein 25.5g, Carbs 8g, Fat 17.6g

Keto Cheesy Lasagna Noodles

Preparation Time: 30 minutes

Cook Time: 40 minutes

Serves: 4 servings

Ingredients (noodles)

1/4 teaspoon onion powder

1/4 teaspoon garlic powder

1/4 teaspoon Italian seasoning

1 1/4 cup shredded, mozzarella cheese

1/4 cup grated, parmesan cheese

4 ounces softened, cream cheese

2 large eggs

Filling

1 teaspoon Italian seasoning

1 teaspoon dried basil

1 teaspoon garlic powder

1 teaspoon oregano, dried

1 tablespoon onion flakes, minced

6 tablespoons whole milk ricotta cheese

3/4 cup shredded, mozzarella cheese

1 1/2 cups (divided) Three Cheese Marinara Sauce

1 pound beef (ground)

Directions

1. Use a parchment paper to line a 13-by-9" baking dish and heat up the oven to 375°F.

2. Add eggs and cream cheese into a big bowl. Use a hand mixer to whisk the mixture together.

3. Add in onion powder, garlic, Italian seasoning and parmesan cheese into the cream cheese bowl.

4. Stir the mixture to combine.

5. Add in the shredded mozzarella cheese to the bowl and stir until combined.

6. Evenly layer the mixture into the baking dish and spread.

7. Place the baking dish on the center rack of the oven. For 20 minutes to 25 minutes, bake noodles.

8. Transfer the cooked noodles into the refrigerator to chill for 20 minutes before cutting the noodles into three.

9. At med-heat, place a big pan over heat. Add salt (a pinch), basil, garlic powder, oregano, onion and ground beef to the pan.

10. Saute mixture until the ground beef becomes golden.

11. Get rid of excess fat from the pan.

12. At low-heat, add marinara sauce (3/4 cup) into beef mixture and simmer the sauce with the beef, for 10 minutes.

13. In a loaf pan, transfer the sauce (1/4 cup) to the base of the pan and add a noddle layer over the sauce.

14. Add beef mixture (1/3 cup) over the noodles, ricotta cheese (3 tablespoons) and mozzarella cheese (1/4 cup).

15. Add the second layer of the noodles over the mozzarella cheese, add beef mixture, ricotta cheese (3 tablespoons) and mozzarella cheese (1/4 cup).

16. Add the third layer of the noodles, the mozzarella cheese and beef mixture that remains.

17. Season the top with Italian seasoning and transfer into the oven for 20 minutes to bake.

Nutritional Information/Serving

Calories 486 kcal, Net Carbs 9.5g, Protein 57g, Fat 34g

Cauliflower Cheddar Casserole

Preparation Time: 10 minutes

Cook Time: 20 minutes

Serves: 8 servings

Ingredients

1/4 cup (chopped) green onions

6 tablespoons (cooked) bacon bits

1 1/2 cup (shredded) cheddar cheese

2 cloves (minced) garlic

1/4 cup heavy cream

2/3 cup sour cream

Black pepper

Sea salt

2 tablespoons (melted) butter

1 large (cut into small florets) cauliflower head

Directions

1. Heat up the oven to 450°F.

2. Add the cauliflower florets and butter into a big bowl.

3. Toss to coat the florets, sprinkle black pepper and salt over the florets to season.

4. In a casserole dish of 1.4 litres, move the coated cauliflower into the dish and arrange in a layer.

Note: If the coated cauliflower seems too much for the casserole dish, use a big lined baking sheet and arrange it in a layer.

5. Transfer the casserole dish into the oven and bake until it is soft and crispy for 15 minutes to 20 minutes.

6. Add heavy cream and sour cream into a small bowl and whisk the creams together until a fine texture is reached.

7. Divide the green onions, bacon bits and cheddar cheese into half.

8. Add in green onions (half), 3 tablespoons of bacon bits, cheddar cheese (half) and garlic into the sour cream bowl.

9. Sprinkle black pepper and salt over the sauce mixture in the bowl as needed.

10. Remove the casserole dish from the oven and don't put off the oven.

11. Add in the baked cauliflower to the sauce bowl and stir together.

12. In the same dish used to bake the cauliflower, return the cauliflower mixture and add in 3 tablespoons of bacon bits and the remaining cheddar cheese into the casserole dish.

13. Transfer the casserole dish into the oven and bake until the cheese melts for 5 minutes to 10 minutes.

14. Add the remaining green onions to top cauliflower.

Nutritional Information/Serving

Calories 231 kcal, Dietary Fiber 3g, Net Carbs 4g, Protein 10g, Fat 18g

Keto Oxtail Stew

Preparation Time: 10 minutes

Cook Time: 2 hours

Serves: 6 servings

Ingredients

Waters

Salt

15 oz can (rinsed & drained) butter beans

1 tsp curry

1 tbsp Worcestershire sauce

5-6 Whole pimento seeds

2 (chopped) green onions

1 whole scotch bonnet pepper

1 tbsp ketchup

½ tsp paprika (smoked)

1 tsp fresh thyme (chopped)

2 tsps garlic (minced)

1 (chopped) onion

1-2 lbs. (cut up medium pieces) oxtail

2-3 tablespoon cooking oil

Directions

1. Add oxtail into a bowl.

2. Sprinkle pepper and salt over the oxtail to season, and let stand.

3. At med-heat, place a big pot over heat and add cooking oil.

4. Heat the cooking oil and add in the seasoned oxtail.

5. Saute oxtail and stir until it is golden.

6. Add paprika, Worcestershire sauce, whole pimento seeds, fresh thyme, minced garlic, green onions and onions into the pot with the oxtail.

7. Stir-cook for 1 minute and add in curry powder, ketchup and scotch bonnet pepper into the oxtail mixture.

8. Stir-cook for another 1 minute.

9. Add in 4 cups to 6 cups of water into the oxtail mixture and boil.

10. Simmer and stir-cook for 1 hour 40 minutes to 2 hours, until the oxtail becomes soft.

11. Add in the drained butter beans into the oxtail mixture and cook for 20 minutes.

12. Thin out the oxtail soup with water as needed, if the soup is too thick.

13. Sprinkle salt into the soup as desired.

Nutritional Information/Serving

Calories 470 kcal, Protein 50g, Dietary Fiber 4g, Carbohydrates 14g, Fat 22g

Caribbean Keto Pepper Pot

Preparation Time: 15 minutes

Cook Time: 2 hours 30 minutes

Serves: 5 servings

Ingredients (pepper pot)

Pepper

Salt

1 cinnamon stick (divided)

3 cups water

¾ – 1 cup cassareep

1 scotch bonnet pepper

2 tsps (minced) fresh thyme

2 (diced) green onions

1 medium (chopped) onion

2 -3 cloves (minced) garlic

1-2 tbsps brown sugar substitute for keto

Marinate oxtail

1 tsp bouillon powder

½ medium (large diced) onion

1 tsp white pepper

1 tsp thyme

1 tsp garlic (minced)

Salt

4 pounds meat (Oxtail) cut into chunks

Directions

1. In a big bowl, add oxtail chunks, bouillon powder, diced onion, white pepper, minced thyme, minced garlic and salt.

2. Use your hand to mix the oxtail mixture well covered and coated.

3. Place the oxtail bowl into the refrigerator to marinate.

Note: Marinate for 8 hours.

4. Remove the marinated oxtail from the refrigerator and shake off the excess spice.

5. At med-heat, place a big cast-iron skillet over heat and add in the brown sugar substitute.

6. Stir-cook until the sugar substitute starts to turn deep golden and is caramelized.

7. Add in the marinated oxtail, stir and cook for 3 minutes until it is brown.

8. Transfer the oxtail onto a plate.

9. In a cast-iron skillet, add in scotch bonnet pepper, minced thyme, chopped onion and minced garlic.

10. Saute the onion mixture, for 3 minutes to 5 minutes, and add in 1/2 cup of cassareep into the skillet.

11. Mix thoroughly and cook for a minute to 2 minutes.

12. Add in 3 cups of water into the cassareep mixture, boil and simmer for 40 minutes.

13. Add the remaining cassareep and the cooked oxtail into the skillet. Add in additional water if desired.

14. Cook until the oxtail is soft for 1 hour 30 minutes to 2 hours.

Note: The oxtail should be soft and the sauce must be thick.

15. Taste and add more seasoning if needed.

16. Serve with bread and top with parsley.

Nutritional Information/Serving

Calories 926 kcal, Protein 112g, Dietary Fiber 1g, Carbohydrates 7g, Fat 48g

Mongolian Keto Beef

Preparation Time: 15 minutes

Cook Time: 10 minutes

Serves: 4 servings

Ingredients (marinade)

2 cloves (chopped) garlic

1 tsp (grated) ginger

1/4 cup coconut aminos

Steak

3 green onions (slice into 1" long diagonal slices)

1/4 cup coconut Oil

1 pound (sliced thinly against the grain) flat Iron steak

Directions

1. In a small ziploc bag, add in the flat iron steak, chopped garlic, grated ginger and coconut aminos.

2. Seal the ziploc bag, shake and transfer into the refrigerator for an hour to marinate.

3. Remove the steak from the ziploc bag, drain the liquid and reserve it.

4. Place a cast-iron skillet over heat and add in coconut oil.

5. Heat the coconut oil until it is nearly smoky.

6. Add in the drained steak into the heated coconut oil.

7. Stir and saute for a minute to 3 minutes on high-heat.

Note: Saute the steak in two batches to prevent crowding the skillet.

8. Add in sliced green onions into the skillet with the steak and saute for 30 seconds to a minute.

9. Serve steak.

Nutritional Information/Serving

Calories 337 kcal, Protein 21g, Carbohydrates 4g, Fat 25g, Net Carbs 4g, Dietary Fiber 0.8g

Delicious Parmesan Cheddar Crisps

Preparation Time: 5 minutes

Cook Time: 7 minutes

Serves: 4 servings

Ingredients

1 teaspoon Italian seasoning

3/4 cup (shredded) cheddar cheese

3/4 cup (shredded) parmesan cheese

Directions

1. Use parchment paper to line a big baking pan and heat up the oven to 400°F.

2. In a small bowl, add the cheddar cheese and parmesan cheese. Stir together.

3. Evenly scoop cheeses in small heaps onto the prepared baking pan and leave 5cm space between each cheese heap.

4. Season the cheeses with Italian seasoning and transfer the baking pan into the prepared oven.

5. Bake the cheeses until the ends are just golden for 6 minutes to 8 minutes.

6. Remove the pan from the oven and set aside to cool.

7. Pat dry the crisps on a paper towel and serve.

Nutritional Information/Serving

Calories 152 kcal, Dietary Fiber 0g, Net Carbs 1g, Protein 11g, Fat 11g

Keto-Japanese Sushi Rolls

Preparation Time: 15 minutes

Cook Time: 0 minutes

Serves: 5 servings

Ingredients

Cold water

20 sheets seaweed snacks

1/2 medium avocado (cut into 20 pieces of 1/4" thick and wider)

1/2 medium (8 inches long) cucumber (slice into 1/4" thick)

1/4 large red bell pepper (slice into 1/4" thick)

4 ounces smoked salmon (cut into 20 pieces of 1/4" thick and wider)

Directions

1. Cut the seaweed snacks into 1/4" length on the narrow side.

2. On a cutting board, lay five seaweed snacks in a layer.

3. In a bowl, add cold water and dip your fingers into the cold water. Place your wet fingers on each seaweed sheet (short ends only), to line it.

4. At the opposite ends of the seaweed snacks, place each piece of avocado, cucumber, red pepper and salmon.

5. Lay 5 more seaweed snacks in a single layer on the same cutting board (arrange in row).

6. Roll the seaweed snacks and seal by pressing the wet ends.

7. On a plate, add in the rolled sushi, seam-side down and repeat the above process with the remaining seaweeds snacks.

Nutritional Information/Serving

Calories 80 kcal, Dietary Fiber 2g, Net Carbs 2g, Protein 6g, Fat 5g

Tasty (No-Sugar) Marshmallows Recipe

Preparation Time: 15 minutes

Cook Time: 5 minutes

Serves: 16 servings

Ingredients

2 teaspoons vanilla extract

1/4 teaspoon sea salt

1/2 teaspoon vanilla liquid stevia

1 1/2 cup sweetener (powdered)

1 cup (warm) water

2 tablespoons gelatin powder (unflavored)

Directions

1. Use a parchment paper to line a 20 by 20 cm baking sheet and let stand.

2. In a big bowl, add warm water (1/2 cup) and sprinkle the 2 tablespoons of unflavored gelatin powder into the water.

3. Whisk the gelatin mixture together immediately and let stand.

4. In a big saucepan, add in salt, liquid stevia, sweetener and the remaining warm water.

5. Place the saucepan with the sweetener mixture over med-heat, stir-cook until the sweetener dissolves and it is almost boiling for few minutes.

Note: The mixture will change color to lightly translucent, and then put off the heat once it starts releasing bubbles at the ends.

6. Add in the vanilla extract into the mixture in the saucepan.

7. Transfer the cooked sweetener mixture into the gelatin bowl.

8. Beat the sweetener mixture in the bowl with a hand mixer for 12 minutes to 15 minutes on high power, until the mixture becomes fluffy and is increased in size.

9. On the lined baking sheet, transfer the marshmallow mixture and place into the fridge until it is solid for 8 hours.

10. Cut into the squares with a knife.

Nutritional Information/Serving

Calories 6 kcal, Dietary Fiber 0g, Net Carbs 0.1g, Protein 1g, Fat 0g

Cheesy Ham Roll ups

Preparation Time: 15 minutes

Cook Time: 0 minutes

Serves: 4 servings

Ingredients

3 medium (cut into 3" pieces) green onions

1/2 cup dill pickle spears

6 ounces (slices) ham

4 ounces cream cheese

Directions

1. On a ham slice, add a tablespoon of cream cheese and spread.

2. On the edge of each ham slice, add green onions and pickle.

3. Form a tube shape by rolling the ham slices and filling.

4. Slice each ham roll into four equal pieces and insert a toothpick to secure each piece.

Nutritional Information/Serving

Calories 171 kcal, Dietary Fiber 1g, Net Carbs 2g, Protein 9g, Fat 14g

Keto Egg Muffins

Preparation Time: 10 minutes

Cook Time: 35 minutes

Serves: 12 servings

Ingredients

1/2 teaspoon black pepper

1 teaspoon sea salt

1/4 cup heavy cream

8 large egg

2 tablespoons olive oil

2 cloves (minced) garlic

1 cup (chopped into 1/2-inch pieces) red bell pepper

1 cup (slice into 1/2-inch florets) cauliflower

1 cup (slice into 1/2-inch florets) broccoli

Directions

1. Use parchment paper to line a baking pan and heat up the oven to 400°F.

2. Use silicone muffin liners to line 12 muffin cups.

3. Add olive oil, garlic, red pepper, cauliflower and broccoli into a big bowl and toss together.

4. On the prepared baking pan, add the veggies and arrange in a layer.

5. Transfer the baking pan into the oven and bake until the broccoli ends are golden for 15 minutes to 20 minutes.

6. Turn off the oven, after baking the veggies.

7. In the prepared muffin cups, evenly lay in the vegetables.

8. In a bowl, add the black pepper, salt, coconut cream and eggs. Whisk the egg mixture together.

9. Top veggies in the muffin cups with the egg mixture.

10. Transfer into the oven and bake until eggs are set for 15 minutes to 20 minutes

Nutritional Information/Serving

Calories 88 kcal, Dietary Fiber 1g, Net Carbs 1g, Protein 5g, Fat 7g

Keto Crock Pot Queso Dip

Preparation Time: 2 minutes

Cook Time: 2 hours

Serves: 13 servings

Ingredients

1 cup Monterey Jack cheese

12 ounces salsa verde

8 ounces (cut into cubes) cream cheese

Directions

1. In a slow cooker, add in the Monterey Jack cheese, salsa verde and cream cheese.

2. Mix the salsa verde mixture together and cook on low, for two and half hours.

3. Whisk and stir the salsa verde mixture, every 30 minutes to dissolve the lumps.

Note: You can also puree the dip after cooking to completely get rid of the lumps.

Nutritional Information/Serving

Calories 104 kcal, Dietary Fiber 0g, Net Carbs 2g, Protein 3g, Fat 9g

Keto White Chocolate (Sugarless)

Preparation Time: 5 minutes

Cook Time: 5 minutes

Serves: 8 servings

Ingredients

1/16 teaspoon sea salt

1/2 teaspoon vanilla extract

1/4 cup whole milk powder

1/4 cup erythritol (powdered)

1/4 teaspoon liquid sunflower lecithin

3 tablespoons coconut oil

3 ounces cocoa butter (cut into small pieces of 1/2")

Directions

1. In a small saucepan, add the sunflower lecithin, coconut oil and cocoa butter.

2. On a very low-heat, place the saucepan over heat until the cocoa butter melts. Remove cocoa butter mixture from heat.

Note: The cocoa butter mixture should not boil or simmer.

3. Add in the powdered erythritol into the saucepan and stir until it dissolves.

4. Add salt, vanilla extract and whole milk powder into the cocoa butter mixture.

5. Stir until a fine texture is reached.

6. Use parchment paper to line a small pan and pour the cocoa butter mixture onto it.

7. Place the pan into a refrigerator and refrigerate until the chocolate is solid.

Nutritional Information/Serving

Calories 169 kcal, Dietary Fiber 0g, Net Carbs 0.5g, Protein 0g, Fat 19g

Kale Chips with Nutritional Yeast

Preparation Time: 5 minutes

Cook Time: 25 minutes

Serves: 4 servings

Ingredients

1/4 teaspoon sea salt

3 tablespoons nutritional yeast

1 tablespoon white vinegar

1 tablespoon olive oil

5 ounces (cut into pieces and remove stem) kale

Directions

1. Use silicone mats to line 2 baking pan and heat up the oven to 300°F.

2. Add white vinegar and olive oil into a big bowl. Whisk the olive oil mixture together.

3. Add in the kale into the olive oil mixture and massage.

4. Add salt and 2 tablespoons of yeast over the kale mixture.

5. Stir the mixture together until it evenly breaks apart.

6. On the lined baking pan, arrange the kale in a layer and sprinkle 1 tablespoon of yeast over the kale.

7. Transfer the baking pan into the oven and bake until the chips are crisped, for 20 minutes to 25 minutes.

Nutritional Information/Serving

Calories 70 kcal, Dietary Fiber 2g, Net Carbs 3g, Protein 5g, Fat 4g

Keto Cheese Peach Danish

Preparation Time: 10 minutes

Cook Time: 20 minutes

Serves: 4 servings

Ingredients (Danish)

1 teaspoon vanilla extract

2 tablespoons (melted) butter

4 large (beaten) eggs

1 pinch sea salt

1 teaspoon baking powder

1/3 cup erythritol

1/2 cup coconut flour

Filling

1/2 large (sliced into very thinly wedges) peach

1 teaspoon vanilla extract

2 tablespoons erythritol

4 ounces cream cheese

Directions

1. Use silicone mat to line a baking pan and heat up the oven to 350°F.

2. In a big bowl, add salt, baking powder, erythritol and coconut flour. Stir the mixture together.

3. Stir in butter, vanilla extract and the beaten eggs into the coconut flour bowl.

4. Stir the mixture together until a dough texture is reached.

Note: The dough texture should be moldable (bendable).

5. Cut and roll the dough into 4 equal parts.

6. Roll each part into a ball shape and place it on the prepared baking pan.

7. Flatten each dough until a 1/4" thinness is reached.

8. Add cream cheese into a bowl and microwave until the cheese stirs easily and is very tender, for 30 seconds to 60 seconds.

9. Add in the erythritol and vanilla extract to the cheese bowl. Stir together.

10. On the prepared pan, add the cheese mixture into it, in little scoops.

11. Add the peach over each cheese scoops and lightly press into it.

12. Transfer the pan into the oven and bake until the Danishes are golden and well cooked, for 20 minutes to 25 minutes.

Nutritional Information/Serving

Calories 271 kcal, Dietary Fiber 6g, Net Carbs 5g, Protein 12g, Fat 22g

Roasted Fish Roulade

Preparation Time: 10 minutes

Cook Time: 10 minutes

Serves: 12 servings

Ingredients

1/4 cup fresh dill

8 ounces (sliced thinly) smoked salmon

8 ounces cream cheese

1/4 teaspoon cream of tartar

4 large egg whites (at room temperature)

Directions

1. Use a silicone baking mat to line a baking pan of 11 by 15". Grease the silicone mat and heat up the oven to 400°F.

2. Add cream of tartar and egg whites into a bowl.

3. Use hand mixer to beat mixture until stiff peaks are formed, on med-low speed.

4. When the egg whites are just frothy, increase the hand mixer speed to high speed.

5. Add the egg-white mixture onto the prepared baking pan and use a spatula to spread evenly.

6. Transfer the baking pan into the oven and bake until mixture is brown, for 8 minutes to 10 minutes.

7. In a bowl, add the cream cheese and place into a microwave, until the cheese is tender for 1 minute.

8. Add in fresh dill and stir until a fine texture is formed.

9. Set the crust aside until lightly cool, and gently use spatula to remove the silicone mat.

10. On the baked crust, add the cream cheese mixture and use a spatula to spread.

11. Lay salmon slices over the cream cheese mixture in a layer.

12. On a big piece of aluminum foil, move the crust with filling and roll the wide ends up.

13. Wrap the big aluminum foil around the salmon roll and transfer into the fridge to stick together for 1 hour.

14. Slice roll into 1/2" thick and serve.

Nutritional Information/Serving

Calories 93 kcal, Dietary Fiber 0g, Net Carbs 0g, Protein 5g, Fat 7g

French liver Pate

Preparation Time: 15 minutes

Cook Time: 25 minutes

Serves: 8 servings

Ingredients

1/2 teaspoon black pepper

1/2 teaspoon sea salt

1 tablespoon (remove leaves from the stalks) fresh thyme

2 cloves (minced) garlic

1 medium (minced) shallot

1/2 cup water

2 tablespoons heavy cream

1/3 cup (softened and unsalted) butter

1/2 pound chicken liver (trim white tissue)

Directions

1. At med-heat, place a skillet over heat and add in butter (1 tbsp) to melt.

2. Add in the minced shallot and garlic to the pan. Saute until aromatic for 1 minute.

3. Add in water, thyme, black pepper, salt and chicken livers into the skillet.

4. Adjust heat, by reducing to a simmer and place a lid over the skillet.

5. Simmer the chicken livers mixture and stir-cook until liver is slightly pink inside and lightly golden on the surface, for 4 minutes to 8 minutes.

6. Remove the skillet from heat and set aside the skillet for 5 minutes. Put Off the heat.

7. Drain the moisture out of the skillet.

8. In a food processor, add the remaining butter, heavy cream and chicken liver mixture.

9. Process until a fine texture is reached, and add in black pepper and salt as desired to taste. Process the chicken liver again.

10. In a ramekin, transfer the processed pate and use a plastic wrap to cover tightly.

Note: The plastic wrap should touch the top part of the pate.

11. Use rubber bands to secure the plastic wrap around the ramekin to make it airtight.

12. Transfer the ramekins into the fridge to chill until it is solid for 8 hours.

Nutritional Information/Serving

Calories 116 kcal, Dietary Fiber 0g, Net Carbs 0g, Protein 5g, Fat 10g

Crumbly Topped Pie Cupcakes

Preparation Time: 15 minutes

Cook Time: 30 minutes

Serves: 10 servings

Ingredients (cupcakes)

1/8 teaspoon sea salt

1/2 cup erythritol

1/2 teaspoon baking powder

p1 tablespoon pumpkin pie spice

6 tablespoons coconut flour

1 teaspoon vanilla extract

2 large eggs

1/2 cup coconut cream

2 cups pumpkin puree

Topping

2 tablespoons (slightly heat to soften) coconut cream

1/4 teaspoon cinnamon

2 tablespoons coconut flour

2 tablespoons erythritol

Directions

1. Line 10 cups in a muffin pan with paper liners and heat up the oven to 350°F.

2. Add vanilla extract, eggs, coconut cream and pumpkin puree into a medium bowl and whisk together.

3. Add salt, baking powder, pumpkin pie spice, erythritol and coconut flour into the pumpkin puree bowl. Stir together.

4. Fill the prepared muffin cups with the batter.

Note: The batter should almost fill the prepared cups.

5. In a small bowl, add cinnamon, coconut flour and erythritol. Mix the topping ingredients together.

6. Add coconut cream into the coconut flour mixture and stir.

7. Use a spoon to break the coconut cream into pieces until a crumbled texture is reached.

Note: Add more coconut cream into the topping mixture if the mixture is too powdery.

8. On the batter in the cups, sprinkle the topping evenly and use the back of a spoon to lightly press the topping into the batter.

9. Transfer the muffin pan into the oven and bake until the cupcakes are set, for 30 minutes.

10. Set aside the muffin pan to cool completely and store in the fridge for 1 hour to chill.

Nutritional Information/Serving

Calories 88 kcal, Sugar 3g, Dietary Fiber 5g, Net Carbs 5g, Protein 4g, Fat 5g

Keto Kale Chips

Preparation Time: 5 minutes

Cook Time: 8 minutes

Serves: 2 servings

Ingredients

1/4 teaspoon pink salt

1/8 teaspoon cayenne

1/4 teaspoon chili powder

1/4 teaspoon cumin

1/2 teaspoon garlic powder

1 1/2 tablespoons nutritional yeast

1 tablespoon avocado oil

2 large stalks kale (removed the leaves)

Directions

1. Use parchment paper to line a big baking pan and let stand. Heat up an oven to 300°F.

2. Slice kale leaves into big pieces, rinse and transfer into a salad spinner to dry the kale leaves.

3. On a paper towel, transfer the kale leaves and pat dry. Note: Make sure kale leaves are well dried.

4. In a bowl, transfer the dried kale leaves and dribble avocado oil (1/2 tbsp) over the kale.

5. Use the tips of your finger to massage the kale leaves with the avocado oil.

6. Season the kale leaves with pink salt, cayenne, chili powder, cumin, garlic powder and nutritional yeast (a tbsp).

7. Add in the remaining avocado oil into the kale leaves mixture.

8. Use oiled hand to gently massage the kale leaves with the seasoning.

9. On the lined baking pan, transfer the kale leaves and arrange in a layer.

10. Sprinkle pink salt as desired and 1/2 tablespoon of yeast over the kale leaves in the baking pan.

11. Transfer the baking pan into the oven and bake for 7 minutes to 9 minutes.

12. Set aside the kale chips in the baking pan to cool for 5 minutes and serve.

Nutritional Information/Serving

Calories 98 kcal, Protein 3g, Dietary Fiber 1g, Carbohydrates 6g, Fat 7g

Ketogenic White Truffles

Preparation Time: 10 minutes

Cook Time: 0 minutes

Serves: 10 servings

Ingredients

1/4 cup pastured collagen peptides (2-3 tbsps more)

1 vanilla seed bean

1 tbsp coconut oil

Salt (pinch)

1/3 cup melted, coconut butter

1 cup macadamia nuts, raw

Directions

1. In a food processor, add the raw macadamia nuts and blend the nuts until a fine texture is formed.

2. Add the melted coconut butter and coconut oil into the food processer with the nuts and blend until a mealy texture is formed.

3. Add in collagen peptides, seed bean and salt into the food processor.

4. Blend the mixture until a doughy texture is formed.

5. Add additional salt and vanilla as desired, after tasting the dough.

6. Make 10 white truffles with the dough and arrange it on a plate.

7. Store in a sealed container and place into the freezer or serve immediately.

Nutritional Information/Serving

Calories 188 kcal, Protein 7.5g, Net Carbs 1.5g, Dietary Fiber 2.5g, Fat 17g

SIDE DISH

Keto Zucchini Gratin

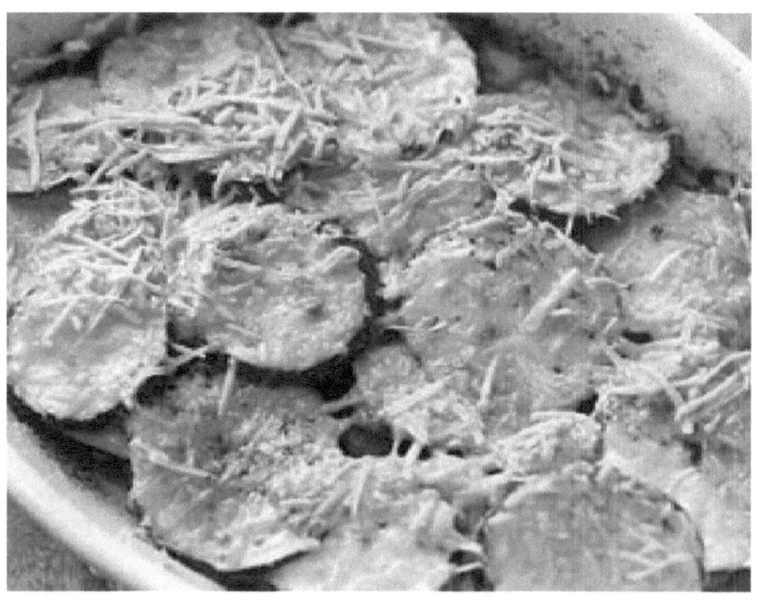

Preparation Time: 10 minutes

Cook Time: 30 minutes

Serves: 6 servings

Ingredients

1/2 tablespoon Italian seasoning

2 cloves (minced) garlic

1 tablespoon butter

2 tablespoons almond milk (unsweetened)

1/3 cup heavy cream

3 ounces brie cheese (ends cut off)

1 1/2 cups sharp cheddar cheese

Black pepper

Sea salt

3 medium zucchinis (sliced into 1/4-inch thin slices)

Directions

1. Add the zucchini slices into a bowl and sprinkle salt over the zucchini slices to season. Toss to coat.

2. Transfer the seasoned zucchini into a colander for 45 minutes to drain.

3. Pat to dry the zucchini. Heat up the oven to 400°F.

4. Lay the zucchini slices in a small casserole dish. Zucchini ends may overlap.

5. Lightly sprinkle black pepper and 3/4 cup of the sharp cheddar cheese over the zucchini slices.

6. In a small saucepan, add the minced garlic, butter, almond milk, heavy cream and brie cheese.

7. At med-low heat, place the saucepan over heat and stir-cook until a fine texture is formed and the cheese melts for few minutes.

8. Sprinkle the brie cheese mixture over the zucchini in the casserole dish.

9. Top the zucchini with the remaining sharp cheddar cheese and Italian seasoning.

10. Transfer the dish into the oven and bake until the zucchini becomes tender and the cheddar cheese is dark brown, for 30 minutes to 35 minutes.

Nutritional Information/Serving

Calories 239 kcal, Dietary Fiber 1g, Net Carbs 5g, Protein 12g, Fat 19g

Easy Ranch Dressing (Keto-Friendly)

Preparation Time: 5 minutes

Cook Time: 0 minutes

Serves: 12 servings

Ingredients

1/4 cup almond milk (unsweetened)

1/4 teaspoon black pepper

1/2 teaspoon sea salt

1/2 teaspoon onion powder

1/2 teaspoon garlic powder

1 teaspoon chives (dried)

1 teaspoon dill (dried)

2 teaspoons parsley (dried)

2 teaspoons lemon juice

1/2 cup sour cream

1 cup mayo

Directions

1. Add black pepper, salt, onion powder, garlic powder, chives, dill, parsley, lemon juice, sour cream and mayo into a bowl and whisk.

2. Gradually add in the unsweetened almond milk into the lemon juice mixture bowl until desired thickness is reached.

Note: More almond milk will give a thinner dressing, and less will result to a thicker dressing.

3. Transfer the dressing into the fridge for the flavors to develop, for an hour.

4. Store dressing in the fridge for 10 days.

Nutritional Information/Serving

Calories 156 kcal, Dietary Fiber 0.1g, Net Carbs 0.9g, Protein 0.4g, Fat 17g

Easy Roasted Spaghetti Squash

Preparation Time: 5 minutes

Cook Time: 25 minutes

Serves: 6 servings

Ingredients

Sea salt

4 teaspoons olive oil

1 medium spaghetti squash

Directions

1. Use foil to line a baking pan and heat up the oven to 425°F.

2. On the prepared baking pan, add the spaghetti squash and place the baking pan into the oven.

3. Bake the spaghetti squash for 35 minutes to 45 minutes, and flip after the first 20 minutes of baking.

4. Use a knife to pierce the skin to check for doneness. It is ready when it pierces through easily.

5. Take out the baking pan from the oven and set aside to cool for 10 minutes before cutting.

6. Slice the baked spaghetti squash into two.

7. Remove the baked spaghetti squash seeds and release the strands with a fork.

8. Season with your preferred sauce, olive oil and salt.

9. Toss to coat and serve.

Nutritional Information/Serving

Calories 75 kcal, Dietary Fiber 2g, Net Carbs 8g, Protein 1g, Fat 4g

CONDIMENTS

Keto Sugarless BBQ Sauce

Preparation Time: 5 minutes

Cook Time: 20 minutes

Serves: 20 servings

Ingredients

1 1/2 cup water

1/4 teaspoon cayenne pepper

1/4 teaspoon chili powder

1/2 teaspoon sea salt

1/2 teaspoon onion powder

1 teaspoon garlic powder

2 teaspoons paprika (smoked)

1 tablespoon liquid hickory smoke

2 tablespoons Worcestershire sauce

1/3 cup erythritol (powdered)

1/2 cup apple cider vinegar

2 1/2 (6-ounces) cans tomato paste

Directions

1. In a saucepan, add cayenne pepper, chili powder, salt, onion powder, garlic powder, paprika, liquid hickory smoke, Worcestershire sauce, erythritol, apple cider vinegar and tomato paste.

2. Add in a cup of water into the saucepan and whisk; add the remaining 1/2 cup of water if the sauce is not as thin as desired.

3. Whisk the tomato paste mixture together until it is lightly thicker than a barbecue sauce.

4. At med-heat, place the saucepan with the sauce over heat and lightly boil the sauce.

5. Remove the saucepan lid and simmer until the sauce is slightly thicker, for 20 minutes. Stir frequently.

6. Taste the sauce and add additional cayenne pepper, if you want the sauce to be spicier, or add in more sweetener if you want the sauce to be sweeter.

Note: Thin out the sauce with 1 tbsp of water at a time, if the sauce is thicker than desired.

Nutritional Information/Serving

Calories 20 kcal, Dietary Fiber 1g, Net carbs 3.5g, Protein 1g, Fat 0.1g

Keto Dipping Sauce

Preparation Time: 5 minutes

Cook Time: 0 minutes

Serves: 10 servings

Ingredients

1/4 teaspoon sea salt

1/2 teaspoon cayenne pepper

1 teaspoon oregano (dried)

1 teaspoon paprika

1 teaspoon Worcestershire sauce

1 teaspoon mustard

1 tablespoon horseradish

1 tablespoon ketchup

1/2 cup mayo

Directions

1. Add salt, cayenne pepper, oregano, paprika, Worcestershire sauce, mustard, horseradish, ketchup and mayo into a bowl.

2. Stir the dip until a fine texture is formed.

3. Cover the bowl and place into a fridge until you are ready to serve or for about 30 minutes.

Nutritional Information/Serving

Calories 91 kcal, Dietary Fiber 0.1g, Net Carbs 0.9g, Protein 0.1g, Fat 10g

Mexican Enchilada Sauce

Preparation Time: 5 minutes

Cook Time: 10 minutes

Serves: 8 servings

Ingredients

1/2 teaspoon sea salt

1 teaspoon onion powder

2 teaspoons cumin

2 teaspoons oregano (dried)

2 tablespoons chili powder

15 ounces tomato sauce

1/2 cup vegetable broth

4 cloves (minced) garlic

1 teaspoon coconut oil

Black pepper

Directions

1. At med-heat, place a medium saucepan over heat and add coconut oil.

2. Add in the minced garlic and cook until it is aromatic for 1 minute.

3. Add in salt, onion powder, cumin, oregano, chili powder, tomato sauce and vegetable broth into the saucepan with the garlic.

4. Cover the saucepan with lid. For 10 minutes, simmer the tomato sauce mixture.

5. Occasionally stir the sauce until it thickens as desired.

6. Taste and add more black pepper and salt, as desired.

Nutritional Information/Serving

Calories 34 kcal, Dietary Fiber 2g, Net Carbs 4g, Protein 1g, Fat 1g

Keto Maple Syrup

Preparation Time: 5 minutes

Cook Time: 5 minutes

Serves: 8 servings

Ingredients

1/2 teaspoon xanthan gum

1 1/2 tablespoons maple extract

1 cup erythritol (powdered)

1 cup water

Directions

1. In a small saucepan, add maple extract, erythritol and water. Whisk together.

2. Lightly boil the erythritol mixture and reduce the heat to simmer.

3. Stir the mixture until powdered erythritol dissolves, for 5 minutes.

4. In a blender, transfer the erythritol mixture and lightly sprinkle with 1/4 teaspoon xanthan gum.

5. Puree the mixture immediately until the lump dissolves.

6. Set aside the pureed mixture to thicken for a few minutes.

Note: To thin out if you desire, sprinkle 1/16 teaspoon of xanthan gum per time and puree in the blender again, until desired thickness is reached.

Nutritional Information/Serving

Calories 1 kcal, Protein 0.0g, Carbs 24.2g Dietary Fiber 0.2g, Fat 0.0g

Keto Cranberry Sauce

Preparation Time: 5 minutes

Cook Time: 10 minutes

Serves: 6 servings

Ingredients

1/2 teaspoon vanilla extract

1 teaspoon orange zest

3/4 cup water

1 cup erythritol (powdered)

12 ounces cranberries

Directions

1. In a medium saucepan, add orange zest, erythritol, water and cranberries.

2. Boil the cranberry mixture.

3. Simmer on low-heat until the cranberries pops and sauce is formed, for 10 minutes to 15 minutes.

4. Take off saucepan from heat and add in vanilla extract.

5. Stir together.

Nutritional Information/Serving

Calories 32 kcal, Dietary Fiber 2g, Net Carbs 4g, Protein 0g, Fat 0g

Keto-Friendly Alfredo Sauce

Preparation Time: 10 minutes

Cook Time: 10 minutes

Serves: 6 servings

Ingredients

Nutmeg

Sea salt

Black pepper

1/2 cup parmesan cheese (grated)

1 1/2 cup heavy cream

6 cloves (minced) garlic

1 tablespoon butter

Directions

1. At med-heat, place a medium saucepan over heat and add butter.

2. Add in garlic and cook until aromatic for 30 seconds.

3. Add heavy cream into the saucepan, simmer the mixture until it reduce in size and starts to thicken for 5 minutes.

4. At low-heat, add in the grated parmesan cheese and whisk until a fine texture is formed.

5. Season the sauce with black pepper and salt as desired.

Note: Thin out the sauce with additional heavy cream if it is too thick.

Nutritional Information/Serving

Calories 253 kcal, Dietary Fiber 0g, Net Carbs 3g, Protein 3g, Fat 25g

END

Thank you for reading my book.

Dolores Hearn